JESUS, PAUL AND JUDAISM

An Introduction to New Testament Theology

JESUS, PAUL AND JUDAISM

An Introduction to
New Testament Theology

by

LEONHARD GOPPELT
Professor of New Testament Theology
University of Hamburg

English edition translated and edited by Edward
Schroeder, Assistant Professor of Theology
Valparaiso University, Valparaiso, Indiana

THOMAS NELSON & SONS

London NEW YORK *Toronto*

This English translation represents the first half of Leonhard Goppelt, Christentum und Judentum im ersten und zweiten Jahrhundert, ein Aufriß der Urgeschichte der Kirche. C. Bertelsmann Verlag, Gütersloh, 1954, revised by the author and translated by Edward Schroeder

Library of Congress Catalog Card Number: 64-25284

Printed in the United States of America

Foreword

The most promising avenue for grasping the meaning of the individual assertions of the New Testament and the Christian faith is to gain a comprehensive picture of the earthly ministry of Jesus and the beginnings of the church and its proclamation. To develop such a comprehensive picture is the intent of this book. It seeks to draw the chief contours of such a composite view by looking at that historico-theological problem which is at the heart of Jesus' career as well as that of the primitive church, namely, their controversy with Judaism. Not all the individual component elements of Jesus' ministry and the primitive church's development can be included, but the basic and essential outlines can be seen by following this critical controversy. Precisely for this reason this book can serve as an introduction to New Testament theology. The particular approach to this central problem is discussed in the Introduction.

The only possible contemporary way to arrive at a picture of Jesus' career and that of the primitive church is both to utilize historical biblical scholarship and at the same time to engage in critical debate with it. Since historical biblical scholarship arose from the world view characteristic of the post-enlightenment age, it is always in danger of viewing Jesus and the primitive church through the glasses of this modern world view. We seek to make positive use of historical research and yet to understand Jesus and the primitive church in terms of their own conscious self-awareness. It must be remembered, of course, that in their own day the Jewish and Hellenistic environment saw in Jesus and the

5

church a phenomenon quite different from this conscious self-awareness. And even today a man's view of Jesus and the primitive church depends in large measure upon his own particular philosophico-theological stance and not merely upon the depth of his scholarly historical penetration.

When this book originally appeared in German in 1954, it represented a distinct counter-proposal to the overall view of Jesus and the early church associated with Bultmann, which largely dominated Germany at that time. The generally friendly reception which this counter-proposal has received from biblical scholars is reported in the foreword to the French translation made by Prof. Pierre Bonnard of Lausanne and published by Payot (Paris).

Shortly after the publication of the German edition Edward Schroeder translated the most important sections into English for use by students of Valparaiso University as introductory material to the study of Jesus and the early church. By virtue of his faithful assistance, for which I am very grateful, the first half of the entire German monograph has been re-worked to produce the present book. Biblical research which has occurred during the decade since the book's first appearance has been utilized for this English text and the footnotes have been revised to make use of the English literature on the subject. In referring the theologically interested reader to other works for more detailed study of specific problems, care has been taken to select such as will give him the best access to the more recent research and discussion of such issues.

It is my wish that within the English-speaking world students and all others who have a concern for theological comprehension of Jesus and the primitive church up through the age of St. Paul may find this book an honest and useful introductory tool for that very task.

Hamburg, Easter, 1964   L. Goppelt

Contents

9

Abbreviations

Billerbeck   STRACK, H. L. and BILLERBECK, P. Kommentar zum Testament aus Talmud und Midrasch. I-V. München, 1922ff.

Moore   MOORE, G. F. *Judaism in the First Centuries of the Christian Era.* I-III. (2nd ed.) Cambridge, 1950

ThLZ   *Theologische Literaturzietung*

ThR   *Theologische Rundschau*

TWNT   KITTEL, G. and FRIEDRICH, G. (eds.) *Theologisches Wörterbuch zum Neuen Testament.* I-VI

ZNW   *Zeitschrift für Neutestamentliche Wissenschaft*

ZThK   *Zeitschrift für Theologie und Kirche*

JESUS, PAUL AND JUDAISM

An Introduction to New Testament Theology

INTRODUCTION

Chapter I

Concerning Problem and Method

Jesus appears in history within the context of Judaism. His work occurred amidst the Jews and was progressively shaped by the controversy he had with them. The same applies to primitive Christianity. This connection with Judaism is not merely a historical accident as the gnostics of the second century were already asserting, but as Jesus and the whole New Testament view it, it is a *heilsgeschichtlich* connection, a purposeful connection within the redemptive history that God has planned. Jesus is not the founder of a new religion, who might just as well have arisen in Athens or Rome, but he is the promised One who completes God's covenant with Israel. By the same token the church is "the Israel of God," the people of the new covenant promised to Israel. For this reason the relationship of Jesus and primitive Christianity to Judaism is for us not only the historical problem, but also the theological problem whose solution will fundamentally condition how we understand Jesus and the New Testament.

There are a *variety of perspectives* from which one can investigate the relationship of Jesus and primitive Christianity to Judaism. The *perspective we wish to follow* because it appears the most important to us is expressed in the question: How did Jesus and the teachers of primitive Christianity themselves view their relationship to Judaism; what posture did they assume in confrontation with Judaism; and how did this shape the subsequent development of the controversy between both of them? We can arrive at an answer to this question by mining the sources, primarily the New Testament documents, historically and exegetically. In essence our question is therefore a question in New Testament theology.

However, two other questions arise alongside or even behind the one we have asked. If we are to understand the posture of Jesus and primitive Christianity toward Judaism, we must come to terms with the *issue raised by history of religions* and *history of traditions*: To what extent did Jesus and primitive Christianity appropriate from the various movements within Judaism their theological concepts and ideas, doctrinal affirmations, thought patterns and forms of expression, patterns of piety, and so forth? This issue confronts New Testament scholarship with an endless task. Simply the investigation of the connections in conceptual history has already filled several thousand pages of the *Theologisches Wörterbuch zum Neuen Testament* (*TWNT*) founded by G. Kittel. We can only entertain this issue to the degree that it is indispensable for clarifying our own specific theme. To what extent that is necessary also depends upon historico-theological judgments. For example, if we considered Jesus to be an apocalyptic preacher or an offshoot of the Essenes and sought to explain His relationship to His surroundings from this perspective, then we would spend more time investigating His historical associations with the traditions of those movements than we would if we had other judgments about His religious affiliations.

The issue raised by history of religions and history of traditions is one we must neither overestimate nor underestimate. The issue was raised and developed by the historical thinking characteristic of modern times. This reflection upon history engendered the historical Biblical research in the eighteenth century. The New Testament itself, however, gives theological impetus to such an issue, for the

16

Logos of God became "flesh" in Jesus (Jn 1.14), a first-century Jewish man. But to be a man means to be enmeshed in history (Gal 4.4). When we address the issue raised by history of religions we attempt to understand Jesus and primitive Christianity as far as possible as the product of a historical development. But we dare not fall prey thereby to the materialistic philosophy of history and suppose that we can and must explain Jesus and the development of the church "purely historically," as Troeltsch said, as though they represented a sort of "chemical mixture" or a "biological progression" of existing religious movements. We must forget neither the limitations of purely historical explanations of which modern philosophy of history reminds us, nor by any means the theological relation between revelation and history, between reason and the knowledge of faith of which the Bible keeps us mindful. In this way we are guarded against relapsing either into the perspective of liberalism, which viewed Jesus individualistically as a "religious personality," or into that supernaturalism that explained everything as stemming from transcendent revelation. Instead we achieve a freedom for evaluating both historically and theologically the uniqueness of Jesus and primitive Christianity vis-à-vis their surroundings.

These hermeneutic reflections also apply to another issue. If we wish to evaluate the posture assumed by Jesus and primitive Christianity in their relationship to Judaism and determine its place in history, we have to test it according to the *methods of comparative religions*. Both Jesus and His Jewish opponents always viewed each other subjectively. The evangelists always present Jesus' controversy with the Jews from the point of view of their own faith and their own experience. The modern historian of religion seeks to determine objectively the relationship between Jesus and the Jews and he takes into consideration not only their actual statements to and about each other but other

17

assertions as well. In this manner, for example, contemporary Jewish historians of religion have sought to demonstrate that Pauline theology has a different relationship to Jewish theology than Paul himself supposed. In addition, the discipline of comparative religions compares certain manifestations of religions, even if these never actually confronted one another. Thus, for example, the ethics of Jesus are compared with rabbinic ethics or, more recently, with the ethics of the Essenes.

Without a doubt this approach is historically and theologically necessary and illuminating. But in such work the investigator must remain hermeneutically open to the fact that every comparison of religions, as soon as it gets beyond mere statistics, is inevitably conditioned by one's own point of view, and for this reason he must constantly remind himself of the principles and presuppositions on which his own judgments are based.

In our own investigation we will limit our use of comparative religions to whatever is necessary for historically and theologically ordering and evaluating the controversy of Jesus and primitive Christianity with Judaism. We will preface this with a historical survey of the religious structure of that Judaism within which Jesus Himself appeared. In addition, we shall address the question (as far as it is necessary and possible) whether the posture assumed by Jesus and the church toward Judaism was justified by the historical situation insofar as we know it from non-Christian, primarily Jewish, sources. By contrast we will, for example, seldom compare Jesus with the Essenes, and then only for illustrative purposes, because He never said anything about His relationship with them. Both geographically and in theological content the Essenes were for Jesus too far out on the periphery of Judaism.

Of course, we shall not be able to present every aspect of the relationship of Jesus and the early church to Judaism,

18

but we hope to work out the elements that are historically and theologically essential, namely, those inherent in the actual controversy of Jesus and the early church with Judaism. We want to trace the development of this controversy up to that point when church and synagogue clearly split apart from each other, at the end of the Pauline era. The development of this controversy lets us see the direction and the turning points of the path which Jesus and the inchoate church followed. This development up until the Pauline era actually constitutes the main thread of New Testament theology.

Our question comes up for consideration therefore in all scholarly works dealing with Jesus, the history of the apostolic age, and New Testament theology, but the treatment is insufficient. In these works Jesus' controversy with the Pharisees or Paul's posture toward Israel in Rom 9-11 appear too peripheral. More significant special investigations of our question have just recently appeared,[1] but their concern with the issue is focused on the current encounter between Christians and Jews. Our concern is a strict investigation of the question in terms of New Testament theology in order to find a historico-theological access to understanding Jesus and the growth of the church and its gospel, and in this fashion to be of service to the kerygma today, including the confrontation with contemporary Israel.

[1] Jakob Jocz, *The Jewish People and Jesus Christ, A Study in the Controversy Between Church and Synagogue* (2d ed.; London, 1954). James Parkes, *The Foundations of Judaism and Christianity* (London, 1960). W. D. Marsch and K. Thieme (eds.), *Christen und Juden. Ihr Gegenüber vom Apostelkonzil bis heute* (Göttingen, 1961).

Chapter II

Judaism at the Time of Jesus[1]

1. The Rise of Judaism[2]

Judaism is not "the religion of the Old Testament."
Rather it is the way of life of the Jewish people, characterized by a particular way of interpreting the Old Testament
revelation. This interpretation had been developing long
before the Old Testament scriptures were canonized.

The growth of Judaism and the development of the
Old Testament canon mutually affected each other. They
did so in much the same way as the growth of the Catholic
Church and the development of the New Testament canon
affected each other. In both cases, a people of God traced
their origins back to the mighty works of God. But in preserving the record of that origin both of these communities
employed certain principles that were not altogether consistent with the original tradition. In adhering to these distinctive principles of interpretation, both communities
sought to secure their own places in history. But in these acts

---

[1] E. Schürer, Geschichte des jüdischen Volkes im Zeitalter Jesu Christi.
3 vols. (3d and 4th eds.; Leipzig, 1898ff. Eng. transl. of 2d ed., New
York, 1892). A. Schlatter, Geschichte Israels von Alexander d. Gr. bis
Hadrian (Stuttgart, 1925). S. W. Baron, A Social and Religious History of
the Jews. 2 vols. (New York, 1952). W. F. Albright, The Biblical Period
from Abraham to Ezra (4th ed.; New York, 1963). L. Finkelstein (ed.),
The Jews, Their History, Culture, and Religion, Vol. I (New York, 1960).
M. Noth, History of Israel (2d ed.; London, 1960). G. von Rad, Theology
of the Old Testament. 2 vols. (Munich, 1957ff.; vol. I transl. New York,
1962). Concerning the development of the specific Old Testament and
Jewish works mentioned below and the literature pertinent to them, see
O. Eissfeld, Introduction to the Old Testament (London, 1963) and
Peake's Commentary on the Bible, ed. by M. Black and H. H. Rowley
(New York, 1962).

[2] See the discussion in V. Rad, I, 85-102 (English ed.) and II, 419-21
(German ed.).

of preservation, even if they were tinged with self-preservation, they also assured that their testimony to the original revelation—a revelation that exceeded their principles of interpreting it—would carry over from one generation to the next.

Judaism as well as the term Jew came into being during and after the *Babylonian Exile* (587-538 B.C.).[3] There would have been no Judaism had there not first been this loss of national self-government and the subsequent scattered existence of the Jewish people in the *Diaspora* (Dispersion). The Diaspora has, indeed, remained the hallmark of the Jewish people to this day. Not only the external institutions of Judaism but also its internal structures stem from the Exile. In the Exile the prophecy of an Ezekiel and of a Deutero-Isaiah renewed the certainty that Israel had been chosen, "*elected*," *to salvation*, despite all appearances to the contrary. The development of Judaism was very much influenced by the hope of salvation which this prophecy held out to the Jewish people. But Judaism as a religion did not really come into being until this hope of salvation was combined with the idea of *obedience to the Law*, so that salvation came to be seen as a matter of fulfilling the demands of the Law. This was in strong contrast to what the prophets had taught. The whole burden of their message had been that Israel remained God's people chosen for salvation because it could expect God to come to His people's rescue with His grace after He had destroyed them in judgment. There was thus, in the prophets, no optimism at all about Israel's ability to keep the commandments.

[3] This is the traditional viewpoint. M. Noth, *op. cit.*, holds to the contrary (pp. 445f.) that not until Jesus was rejected and the Temple destroyed did Judaism arise. However, the development which does end in talmudic Judaism clearly begins already in the Exile, even if it takes the rejection of the gospel and the demolition of the Temple before it achieves sole dominion within the Jewish people. This is also the position of R. Meyer, "Die Bedeutung des Pharisäismus für Geschichte und Theologie des Judentums," *ThLZ*, LXXVII (1952), 677-84.

Judaism, on the other hand, insisted that Israel remained the chosen people—and that it proved itself to be such—by obeying the commandments and, in return for this obedience, by receiving God's grace from one generation to the next.

What paved the way for this understanding of salvation was the kind of writing recorded in what scholars call the Deuteronomic History of the Old Testament[4] This writing, which was strongly affected by the catastrophic destruction, seems to have been produced during the Exile. It viewed Israel's history not primarily in the light of the final "consummation" or "fulfillment" (eschaton), as the prophets had, but rather from the viewpoint of a transcendent historical law by which God shaped Israel's destiny in pendulum-like fashion with His judgment and His mercy alternatively replacing each other. When the Exile came to an end with the salvation prophesied by Ezekiel and Deutero-Isaiah still unrealized, this particular attitude toward history became embedded in Judaism's very nature. It was then actually formalized during the period when Jewish community life was re-established in Jerusalem after the Exile. We shall briefly examine now the three phases in which this re-establishment proceeded.

1. After conquering the Babylonian empire the Persian king Cyrus ordered in an edict of 538 the *rebuilding* of the *Jerusalem Temple* which the Babylonians had destroyed in 586 (Ezra 6.3-5). However, it was most likely not until the time of his successor Cambyses (529-522) that the citizens of Judah who were exiled in Babylon were able to return to their homeland. And even then it took the prophetic pressure of Haggai and Zechariah to get Temple reconstruction completed. In the spring of 515 this new Temple was dedicated.

2. Seventy years later *Nehemiah* arrived in Jerusalem (444 B.C.). He was responsible for rebuilding the wall of

---

[4] V. Rad, *Theol.* I, 329-344.

the city and thus giving the Jewish community in and around Jerusalem its *political structure* as the independent Persian province of Judea (Neh 1.1-7.5a; 11.1ff.; 12.27-13.31).

3. In all probability it was not until after Nehemiah, around the year 430, that *Ezra*, "the priest and scribe of the God of heaven," appeared on the scene in Jerusalem with special authorization from the Persian king. Ezra pledged the people to the *book of the Law* (Neh 8) and, on the basis of the Law, he forbade the intermarriage of Jews and "outsiders" (Ez 9ff.). By this act, Ezra became the actual founder of Judaism. We can no longer ascertain which of those laws united in the Pentateuch were present in Ezra's "book of the Law." In all probability there was little difference between it and the Pentateuch. At any rate, it directed the Jewish people to the Pentateuch and the Pentateuch soon bcame their Law.

Within the Pentateuch itself, however, the so-called "*priestly code*" predominates. It focuses Israel's history entirely upon God's commands and ordinances and makes of Israel a "cult" religion gathered about the sanctuary, a congregation whose whole round of life is wrapped up by the observance of ritual law. Thus already in the days of the Exile, since cultic worship was impossible in a land which was wholly unclean, Judaism had made a confessional symbol of circumcision and the keeping of the Sabbath (Gen 17.9-14 *P*; Ex 20.12). Very likely it was in the Babylonian Exile that the early beginnings of synagogue worship develop, which we then encounter throughout the entire Diaspora from the third century on (1 Kings 8.46-50). After the time of Ezra it became a basic principle of Judaism that "they made the observance of the laws and the piety thereunto appertaining the most necessary work of their entire life," and "even if we should lose riches, home, and all our goods, at least we still have the indestructible law, and no Jew can ever be so far away from his fatherland or so intimidated by a bitter tyrant that he would cease to respect the Law." (Josephus, c. Ap. 1.60; 2.277.)

Ezra's restriction of Judaism to Jews who were Jewish by birth was immediately countermanded by the acceptance of converts (proselytes) and by intermarriage with them. But the principle of *strict religious and social segregation* from the "outside" remained (2 Macc 19.38). It was this characteristic of Judaism that accounted for the development of the *anti-Semitism* described in the book of Esther, and this anti-Semitism spread throughout the ancient world as the Jewish people themselves were dispersed around the Mediterranean basin. They were "a people scattered abroad and dispersed among the peoples in all the provinces of your kingdom. Their laws are different from those of every other people, and they do not keep the king's laws" (Esther 3.8).[5]

In spite of these basic traits produced by its origins and early growth, Judaism was a complex "personality" that was furthermore strongly conditioned by forces at work in its environment. The real essence of Judaism, though, was this idea that obedience to the Law assured Israel's election—despite all of the historical evidence to the contrary—just as it also assured the promise despite the long delay of its fulfillment. This idea proved to be the principle that more and more shaped the history and the inner structure of the Jewish people. A look at the history of Judaism up until the New Testament era demonstrates this fact.

2. The Development of Judaism Until the Time of Jesus

Even after the establishment of community life around Jerusalem, the majority of the Jewish people remained in

[5] Th. Reinach, *Textes d'auteurs Grecs et Romains relatifs au Judaisme* (Paris, 1895). J. Heinemann, "Antisemitismus," in Pauly-W, Suppl. V, 3-43 (Stuttgart, 1931). V. Tcherikover, *Hellenistic Civilization and the Jews* (Philadelphia & Jerusalem, 1959), pp. 363-77.

their *Diaspora existence*. The community around Jerusalem was never actually the homeland of any considerable part of the Jewish nation—as a matter of fact it was not even a sovereign state except for the few years between 129 and 63 B.C.—but for all Jews everywhere it was the home of their hearts, because the Temple was there. In Babylonia and in Egypt Jewish colonies had been formed as early as the time of the Exile by deportees and refugees from Palestine. By the time Alexander the Great had conquered the lands of the Middle East and inaugurated the age of Hellenization, Jews were to be found everywhere in the Western world— some as a result of mass deportation, some as homesteading prisoners of war, and some as voluntary migrants seeking employment. During the Persian era, Jewish communities had already infiltrated Syria and Asia Minor. Under the Seleucids and the Ptolemies, and later under Roman rule, the process of infiltration continued and Jewish communities arose in all the coastal towns and trading centers of the Mediterranean world. In the early centuries of the Christian Era the Jewish Diaspora extended from Media (modern Iran) to Spain, and from Germany and the Crimea to Ethiopia.[6] In contrast to other folk groups, Judaism maintained its identity as a fellowship bound together by race and religion, even though it used the Greek language almost exclusively. The entire Diaspora proclaimed its affiliation with this fellowship and with its center at Jerusalem by means of the double-drachma Temple tax which every male Jew paid annually. And it confessed its participation in that future which belonged to all of Judaism through its faithfulness to the Law. Indeed it was by the strict practice of the Law that the Diaspora managed to maintain its separateness from alien influences.

The decisive battle between the basic principle of separateness and the opposing principle of absorption into

[6] J. Juster, *Les Juifs dans l'Empire romain* (Paris, 1914), I, 179-212. R. Neher-Bernheim, *Le Judaisme dans le monde romain* (Paris, 1959).

Hellenistic culture was fought *in the mother country.* The Persians had been generally tolerant of Jewish peculiarities, and the Egyptian Ptolemies, to whose kingdom Palestine belonged during the first century of the Hellenistic age (301-206 B.C.), followed the Persian tradition. Precisely because of this generous treatment, Palestinian Judaism accepted Hellenistic culture insofar as the Law permitted. For example, during this century Greek became the second tongue of Palestinian Jews. But when the Syrian Seleucids (205-129 B.C.) attempted to Hellenize the Jews at the expense of their religion they came up against the inner strength of that religion. The attempt by Antiochus Epiphanes IV in 168 to wipe out the law of God by royal edict brought effective retaliation; indeed, the effect of his edict was to mobilize the full strength of Judaism that had been concealed beneath the Hellenization of the upper classes and the vacillation of the masses. From this time dates the prophecy of Daniel, an echo of the Exile prophecies, that promised those who were faithful to the Law and willing to bear martyrdom not only gracious and miraculous help in the present situation but also the imminent replacement of the imperial power by the arrival of the Kingdom of God. The *Maccabees,* a Jewish family of priestly descent, were not content with merely passive demonstrations of faithfulness; they called their countrymen to massive retaliation against the religious oppression of the Syrians. Their successes in battle—greatly aided by internal chaos within the Syrian leadership—gave what seemed to be weighty practical support to the principle that men can accomplish by force of arms objectives which cannot be attained by patient waiting for the grace of God.

Once established in power, the Maccabean high priests themselves soon became Hellenistic petty princes. Thereupon the pious Jews (the Chasidim), who had once supported their battle with the Syrians, united in the party of the *Pharisees* ("separatists") to oppose the Maccabees, and this they did on the basis of the old principle that Judaism's history was shaped by the act of obedience to the Law. After Alexander Jannaeus (103-76 B.C.) had defeated them in a bloody purge, the Pharisees categorically renounced the use of force. But they did not renounce the works of the Law. They continued to hold, on the basis of their belief in the retributive justice of God, that this obedience to the Law would shape the course of history to Israel's salvation. And they carried the day. On his deathbed their old enemy, Alexander Jannaeus, counseled his wife, Alexandra, to make peace with the Pharisees since it had become impossible to rule against their opposition. Thus the champions of unconditional obedience to the Law as the one work that would insure Israel's future achieved moral dominion over the people of the Law.[7] This moral toughness, with its associated renunciation of force as an instrument of power, later earned the Pharisees the high respect of the Romans, for whom they paved the way in Palestine. And when, A.D. 70, Zealotism brought catastrophe upon Jerusalem by again attempting to substitute the sword for obedience to the Law, Pharisaism won exclusive control over the Jewish people. Their principle became the principle of Judaism: total commitment to the zeal that is kindled by the Law because obedience to the Law carried with it the promise. And this dynamic force, which produced Judaism and carved out its place and path in history, also characterized its inner structure. This can be demonstrated by examining a cross-section of Judaism at the beginning of the last chapter of its development, immediately before its encounter with Jesus of Nazareth.

[7] Josephus, *Ant.* 13,10,5: "These are held in such esteem by the people that they are readily believed even when they say something against a king or high priest."

3. The Sociological and Religious Structure of Palestinian Judaism at the Time of Jesus[8]

From the time of the building of the Temple after the Exile until its destruction A.D. 70, the Jewish community was a theocracy. The central representative in this theocracy was the *high priest* whose office was lifelong and hereditary, first in the dynasty of the Zadokites and later in the dynasty of the Hasmonians. Not until the Herodians was the office debased to a temporary honor bestowed arbitrarily on members of a particular clique of priestly families. But the real instrument of Jewish self-government and jurisdiction was the great council—or, to use its Hebrew equivalent, *Sanhedrin*—in Jerusalem. This body, of which the high priest was merely the chairman, was originally made up only of the representatives of the ancient nobility. It was not until the middle of the first century before Christ that this council was enlarged to include scribes from outside its own circle. These scribes were essentially representatives of the Pharisees. The respective places of priest and scribe in this structure of self-government corresponded to their distinctive roles in preserving the Law.

From the beginning, the calling of the *priesthood* was

[8] Cf. note 1 above. R. H. Charles, *Religious Development Between the Old and the New Testaments* (London, 1914). W. Bousset, *Die Religion des Judentums im späthellenistischen Zeitalter* (3d ed.; Tübingen, 1926). P. Volz, *Die Eschatologie der jüdischen Gemeinde im Neutestamentlichen Zeitalter* (2d ed.; Tübingen, 1934). G. F. Moore, *Judaism in the First Centuries of the Christian Era*. 3 vols. (2d ed.; Cambridge, 1950). K. Schubert, *Die Religion des nachbiblischen Judentums* (Freiburg, 1955). J. Jeremias, *Jerusalem zur Zeit Jesu* (2d ed.; Göttingen, 1958). C. K. Barrett, *The New Testament Background, Selected Documents*, ed. with introductions (London, 1956; New York, 1961). M. Simon, *Les sectes juives au temps de Jésus* (Paris, 1960). Important monographs include H. Mantel, *Studies in the History of the Sanhedrin* (Cambridge, Mass., 1961). R. Travers Herford, *The Pharisees* (London and New York, 1924) (in the German translation, *Die Pharisäer* [3d ed.; Cologne, 1961], pp. vii-xxiv give a significant report on research to date). R. Leszinsky, *Die Sadducäer* (Berlin, 1912). W. R. Farmer, *Maccabees, Zealots, and Josephus* (New York, 1956). M. Hengel, *Die Zeloten* (Leiden, 1961).

to preserve the Law and thus to play the leading role in the self-governing Jewish theocracy. The priesthood practiced this calling even into New Testament times. In fact, after the breakdown of the ruling priestly hierarchy, the priesthood itself initiated first the Maccabean and later the Pharisaic movements.

Service in the Temple was a hereditary honor and privilege. Preservation of the Law was not. And so, by the third century before Christ, the *profession of the scribe*, that is, the scripture expert, had branched off from the priesthood as a separate calling. Because of the theocratic character of Jewish common life, the scribe was a combination of lawyer and theologian, representing the Law both in religious instruction and in the executive and judicial branches of government. The scribes' authority was based not only on their knowledge of the written Law but, more especially, on their familiarity with the tradition of the common law and the traditional exegesis of the Torah, i.e., the Halacha,[9] which was passed on verbally from master to pupil.[10] The scribes were the "carriers" of God's will, which was the one unifying bond of the theocracy, and as such they enjoyed the status of successors to the prophets, whose spirit was considered to have vanished at the death of Ezra.

Education and congregational discipline effectively impressed the Law and the Halacha upon *the people*. Beginning at age six every Jewish boy was instructed in reading

[9] Concerning the authority of this tradition the following was taught: "If one . . . cause the Law to bear a meaning other than in accordance with traditional law, then even though knowledge of the Law and good deeds are his, he has no share in the world to come." *Aboth* 3.11; *Mishnayoth*, Vol. IV, ed. by Ph. Blackman (London, 1954), p. 511.

[10] It was not until around A.D. 200 that the orally transmitted Halacha was recorded in the Mishnah. Additional work on the Mishnah produced the Babylonian Talmud around A.D. 450. For an overview of the rabbinic literature see H. L. Strack, *Introduction to the Talmud and Midrash* (New York, 1959). H. L. Strack and P. Billerbeck, *Kommentar zum Neuen Testament aus Talmud und Midrasch* (Munich, 1922ff.). M. Smith, *Tannaitic Parallels to the Gospels* (Philadelphia, 1951).

and writing on the basis of the Torah. The synagogue services, which were reading and preaching services in which each Jew could actively participate as lector or preacher, conveyed to the average Jewish layman a living knowledge of the scriptures and the scribal interpretation of the scriptures. The education was underscored with a stern congregational discipline. Whoever was guilty of public transgression against the law could reckon with a variety of penalties, above all excommunication from the synagogue.

The professional work of the scribes found its counterpart in the religious movement of *Pharisaism*. Pharisaism began as a continuation of the revival of piety (Chasidim) in Maccabean times. It seems probable that at first the Pharisees were members of the priesthood who insisted that the purification ceremonies, which, according to the Pentateuch, applied only to the priests on duty, and the Halacha were binding on all Jews. By New Testament times the Pharisees had become an organized religious fellowship numbering about six thousand with strict conditions of membership and with its own common life, and at the same time a political party whose representatives in the Sanhedrin had the decisive word. The scribes taught the principle of Judaism; the Pharisees practiced it. Thus each movement supported the other. The fellowship of Pharisees claimed to be the holy congregation, the true Israel, and separated themselves from the rest of the people, the unclean "Am-ha-arez." But the separation of the Pharisees was not a matter of snobbish aloofness. Its purpose was to win the whole nation over to their beliefs and way of life, and thereby to make it really God's people. It is not enough to describe Pharisaism as a particular trend in late Judaism; the fact of the matter is that it was the very essence of Judaism. That this was the case is evident from the fact that every other movement in Palestinian Judaism at the time of Jesus was either an extension or parallel of Pharisaism or else an opposition movement to it.

The *Sadducees* traced their origins back to the pro-Hellenistic Judaism of the pre-Maccabean era. They arose from members of the priesthood who rejected the Pharisaic revival for political, social, and ideological reasons. They rejected the Pharisaic doctrines of the binding character of the Halacha and of bodily resurrection. This narrow group, which stemmed from the ecclesiastical and secular nobility, bitterly opposed the Pharisees from Maccabean times on, and finally disappeared from the picture with the destruction of the second Temple in 70.

The Pharisees, trusting in the rewards of righteousness, waited in passive loyalty for God to take a hand against foreign oppressors. The *Zealots*, in all other ways similar to the Pharisees, differed from them in demanding active opposition to foreign rulers. They first appeared on the scene at the time of the census (Lk 2.2). The movement stemmed from a prophet in Galilee known as "Judas the Galilean." In his preaching he asserted that "Israel dare not acknowledge mortal men also as rulers besides God" and therefore dare not pay tax to the Roman emperor (Josephus, *Bell.* 2,8,1). Thus the Zealots became a political resistance movement of religious enthusiasts, a new form of Maccabean activism. To be sure, the entire people prayed daily in the "Prayer of Eighteen Petitions" (Sh'mone-Esre): "Restore to us our judges as before and our magistrates as at the beginning and be thou king over us, thou alone!" But the Zealots wished to achieve this redemption by deeds and not just creeds, while the Pharisees called attention to Dan 2.21 and waited until God Himself should bring this redemption.

In addition to the Zealotic movement and besides the Pharisees and Sadducees, Josephus also mentions the *Es-*

senes.[11] New light has fallen upon this group with the discoveries between 1947 and 1956 in caves at the northwest end of the Dead Sea near Khirbet Qumran of the *Dead Sea Scrolls (DSS).*[12] Among the *DSS* there were, in addition to Biblical manuscripts and other Jewish literature, documents that reveal the theology and the regulations for daily life of a Jewish separatist community. Together with these "sectarian manuscripts" must also be reckoned by virtue of similar content the "Zadokite Fragment" (CD) discovered as early as 1910, and as a matter of fact several fragments of it were found among the *DSS*. The Jewish separatist community that speaks to us from these sectarian documents comes so close in its principles and regulations to the Essenes, of whom Josephus, Philo, and Pliny the Elder speak, that both groups are very likely identical. Even the results of archaeological investigation show that the residents in the buildings and caves of Khirbet Qumran, whose library is represented in the *DSS*, were Essenes. To be sure they never apply this label to themselves. Apparently only outsiders called them such.

If we do call this separatist *DSS* community Essene, we must then envision the Essenes as a group which, although sharply cut off from the outside world (e.g., new members were accepted only after a two-year novitiate), nevertheless internally underwent manifold modifications

[11] *Bell.* 2,8,1-13; *Ant.* 18,1,2-6. Philo, *Quod omnis probus liber*, 75-91. Pliny, *N.H.*, 5,15,4.

[12] For an account of the discovery and research on the scrolls as well as translation of the texts see M. Burrows, *The Dead Sea Scrolls* (New York, 1955) and *More Light on the Dead Sea Scrolls* (New York, 1958). T. H. Gaster, *The Dead Sea Scriptures* (New York, 1956). For historical and theological research in the texts see J. T. Milik, *Ten Years of Discovery in the Wilderness of Judaea* (London, 1959). F. M. Cross, Jr., *The Ancient Library of Qumran and Modern Biblical Studies* (New York, 1958). For bibliography see C. Burchard, *Bibliographie zu den Handschriften vom Toten Meer* (Berlin, 1957) (1556 entries!) and *Ergänzungsband* (Supplement, 1963). W. S. La Sor, *Bibliography of the Dead Sea Scrolls* (Pasadena, 1958).

and variations in the course of its approximately two-hundred-year history. For the community rules and the doctrines which we find in the scrolls and in the reports of the ancient historians are, despite all their similarities, not uniform. The community regulations in the "Manual of Discipline" (*DSD* or 1 *QS*) are considerably different from those in the *CD*. Perhaps the *DSD* represents the regulations of a small inner circle who lived celibately in the "cloister" and caves at Qumran, while the *CD* represents the regulations of the "tertiaries" who were settled in the surrounding area and perhaps elsewhere in the country. But these are very uncertain guesses.

The Essenes, like the Pharisees, arose from the "pious" (Chasidim) of the early Maccabean era. Like the Pharisees the group developed from opposition within the priesthood. One group of priests, perhaps prompted by a pneumatic scribal priest who is called "teacher of righteousness" in the *DSS*, called for a stricter observance of the Law, especially in the cultus, than had been customary up until that time. Consequently they got into serious trouble with the Hasmonean high priest, the "sacrilegious priest" of the *DSS*. Unable to press through their demands they withdrew together with kindred spirits, as 1 *QS* 8. 13-16 says, according to the prophecy of Is 40.3 "into the wilderness," that is, to Qumran, there "to prepare the way" for the impending final coming of God. Apparently the position of the Pharisees struck them as an unsatisfactory compromise. They cut themselves off completely from the desecrated temple in Jerusalem. More thoroughly than the Pharisees they considered themselves exclusively as the true Israel; all other Israelites had fallen and broken the covenant. They alone were the holy "remnant." They were the congregation of the "new covenant" (*CD* 6.19, cf. 15.8ff.; 1 *QS* 5.7ff.), that is, the renewed Sinai covenant, since they alone kept the Torah the way it was really meant to be kept. Spurred

33

on by the teacher of righteousness they interpreted the Torah more radically than the Pharisees, and more completely than the Pharisees they demanded priestly purity for all of life. As required for priests in service they daily purified themselves by immersion (1 QS 3.4-12). As priests lived from the temple service and closed each day's service with a sacrificial meal, so they lived in a fellowship of communal property and ate their meals in common (1 QS 6.4-6, cf. 1 QSa 2.17-22). To some extent they abstained from sexual intercourse just as was the case for the priest during his period of service or the soldiers in a "holy war" (CD 12.1ff). In this fashion they were arming themselves for the holy war of the end-time when God would strike down his enemies. While the Pharisees waited calmly for the temporal and eternal retribution of providence, the Essenes lived in expectation of an immediately imminent interruption of history by God, the coming of "the (two) Messiahs from Aaron and Israel" (1 QS 9.11). They held fast to this expectation of an imminent end for generations although "the last time is lasting a long time" (1 Qp Hab 7.6-14). In addition to these Old Testament traditions a dualism fostered by Iranian influences conditioned their ideas and behavior. For example, they viewed themselves caught in the battle between God and Belial, between "the prince of light" and "the angel of darkness" and knew that they were the "sons of light" while all the rest were "sons of darkness" (1 QS 3.13-4.26).

Related to the Essenes were individual Jewish "Baptists" and Baptist groups mentioned by Josephus and the church fathers.[13] But they seldom report little more than the names, so that about all we know is that in the territory around the Jordan there were other Jewish groups besides the Essenes who placed special value on cleansing rituals

[13] J. Thomas, Le mouvement baptiste en Palestine et Syrie (Gembloux, 1935). K. Rudolph, Die Mandäer I (Göttingen, 1960), pp. 222-31.

34

and immersion. A later development from this Jewish Baptist movement was the Mandeans in Syria.

Among the DSS were also found fragments of already well-known *apocalyptic pseudepigraphs*,[14] for example, of the Ethiopian Enoch. These documents cannot by any means, in view of their theological character, be considered to be of Essene origin. Since the nineteenth century the term "apocalypse" has been the label for a genre of Old Testament-Jewish literature characterized especially by such works as Daniel, Ethiopian and Slavic Enoch, 4 Ezra (2 Esdras) and Apocalypse of Baruch (II Baruch or Syriac Baruch). There are three essential elements in these works, namely, paranesis (admonition), predictions about the course of history for centuries up until the end of the world, and to some extent, cosmological speculation. The predictions are especially characteristic of these works. They present the course of history in the form of visionary pictures making use of a traditional picture language (e.g., Dan 7.2-14). The predictions ostensibly come from a righteous man of antiquity, for example, Enoch; in actuality they come from an author who is himself living face to face with the predicted end. The prediction divides the course of history into a series of periods and portrays the end as cosmic demolition, which is then followed by a new world, the kingdom of God. There are such notions about the end of the world to be found in works that do not belong to this literary genre, for example, in the Testaments of the 12 Patriarchs, in Rabbinic and in primitive Christian literature. Therefore this type of expectation of the end is also frequently called "apocalyptic." But for the sake of clarity the

[14] English translation in R. H. Charles, *The Apocrypha and Pseudepigrapha of the Old Testament* (Oxford, 1913). Investigations include H. H. Rowley, *The Relevance of Apocalyptic* (3d ed.; London, 1955) and *Jewish Apocalyptic and the Dead Sea Scrolls* (London, 1957). M. Black, *On the Apocalyptic in Judaism* (London, 1952). D. Rössler, *Gesetz und Geschichte* (Tübingen, 1960).

35

term ought to be reserved for the literary genre and the views represented in it.

These views taken as a whole do differ considerably from Essene views, but also from Pharisaic-Rabbinic ones. Many scholars have therefore concluded that the apocalypses stem from conventicles of pious laity, "the quiet ones in the land," and were widespread as popular literature. To consider this their *Sitz im Leben*, however, can hardly be accurate. An extensive investigation into the history of the apocalyptic genre and tradition is now just beginning. Until now the following is about all that can be said in general: the Apocalypses originate in esoteric speculation of the scribes. Their authors wish to preserve the heritage of the Old Testament prophets, but they do not place themselves as prophets alongside them. Instead they conceal themselves in scribal fashion behind a tradition ostensibly stemming from antiquity, by means of which they interpret the prophetic writings in their contemporary significance (Dan 9.2). Seen in terms of the history of religions the apocalypses merge statements from Old Testament prophecy with Iranian and Chaldean views. Their notion that the course of history is deterministically fixed from the very beginning into definite periods is, for example, much more akin to Chaldean astral theology than it is to Old Testament prophecy. Just how extensively these works of prophetically inspired teachers were disseminated among the people and among the various religious groups cannot be determined exactly. This much however is known, that in the days of Jesus the Book of Daniel was known and cherished by the whole people (Josephus, *Ant.* 10,1,7).

To round off this overview of Judaism we must call to mind that these distinctive groups within Palestinian Judaism also exerted influence in the Diaspora. In addition to them there was in the western Greek-speaking Diaspora a current which is frequently labeled as *"Hellenistic Juda-*

ism."[15] Its intellectual center was the Jewish Diaspora in Egypt, especially in Alexandria, although its thought and literature (e.g., the first century work, Wisdom of Solomon) permeated the entire Greek-speaking Diaspora. Its greatest achievement was the creation of the Septuagint, that Greek translation of the Old Testament which was gradually produced between the third and first centuries B.C. in Egypt. The Epistle of Aristeas gives the legendary account of its production. The most outstanding representative of Hellenistic Judaism was the Jewish religious philosopher, Philo of Alexandria (approximately 25 B.C. to A.D. 40). The hallmark of Hellenistic Judaism is its attempt to unite Hellenistic culture and philosophy with recognition of the Old Testament, especially of the Law, with a view toward justifying Judaism in the Hellenistic world apologetically both to itself and to its environment. Thus it sought, for example, to explain anthropomorphic Old Testament assertions about God and objectionable ordinances of the law and made use in this very task of the allegorical exegesis developed in Hellenistic philosophy. Palestinian Judaism did not engage the Hellenistic world in this fashion, but neither was it untouched by it, for between the Palestinian mother country and the eastern as well as the western Diaspora a lively exchange of persons and ideas was going on.[16]

Thus Judaism even in Palestine at the beginning of the Christian Era presented an extraordinarily complex picture. It lived in a wide variety of religious views and expectations.

[15] E. R. Goodenough, By Light, Light; The Mystic Gospel of Hellenistic Judaism (Oxford, 1935). P. Dalbert, Die Theologie der hellenistisch-jüdischen Missionsliteratur unter Ausschluss von Philo und Josephus (Hamburg, 1954). H. A. Wolfson, Philo. 2 vols. (Cambridge, Mass., 1947, 1948). J. Daniélou, Philon d'Alexandrie (Paris, 1958). V. Tscherikover, Hellenistic Civilization and the Jews (note 5). R. J. H. Shutt, Studies in Josephus (London, 1961).

[16] S. Liebermann, Greek in Jewish Palestine (New York, 1942); Hellenism in Jewish Palestine (New York, 1950).

Neither then nor to this day did it produce a dogmatics. But it was nevertheless unified by its confession to the God of the Old Testament and by its life under the Law. For this reason the one movement to which the future belonged was that of the Pharisees. This picture of the structure of Judaism is confirmed by its encounter with Jesus and its subsequent history. This encounter shook its very foundations and made its essence transparent.

Part I.

Jesus and Judaism

Preliminary Note on the Sources

Essentially the sources for the history of Jesus[1] are the New Testament documents. Other reports[2] are scarce and generally unreliable. Within the New Testament documents there is a basic difference between the *synoptic gospels* (Matthew, Mark, and Luke) *and the gospel of John.* The first three are various editions of a similar congregational tradition. The gospel of John[3] assumes that the synoptic tradition is well known, but it is itself based on an independent tradition. John's gospel does not seek to displace the synoptic tradition, but seeks to set up its own picture of the earthly career of Jesus and to mediate a better and more profound understanding of this career. It describes extensively what the synoptics briefly hint at, namely, what

[1] See the various presentations on Jesus and the theology of the New Testament. In the older literature A. Schlatter's book, *Die Geschichte des Christus* (Stuttgart, 1923) is very important as is also the picture of Jesus given by the Jewish historians, C. G. Montefiore, *The Synoptic Gospels* 2d ed., 2 vols. (London, 1927), J. Klausner, *Jesus of Nazareth,* Engl. trans. (New York, 1926), and H. J. Schoeps, *Aus frühchristlicher Zeit* (Tübingen, 1950). Cf. G. Lindeskog, *Die Jesusfrage im neuzeitlichen Judentum* (Uppsala, 1938). Among the more recent publications see R. Bultmann, *The Theology of the New Testament.* 2 vols. (New York, 1951 and 1955). M. Dibelius, *Jesus* (Philadelphia, 1949). G. Bornkamm, *Jesus of Nazareth* (New York, 1960). *Peake's Commentary* (Chap. II, note 1) F33-F41.

[2] Concerning other reports, Josephus, the Jewish historian of this epoch (37-38 to approximately A.D. 100), tells us nothing about Jesus. *Ant.* 20,9,1 mentions only the name, while 18,3,3 is most likely an interpolation. The rabbinic writings contain concealed, frequently perverse polemics (*Billerbeck,* IV, 1239, s.v. Jesus). The apocryphal Christian tradition contains hardly any reliable information: See J. Jeremias, *Unknown Sayings of Jesus* (London, 1957). R. M. Grant and D. N. Freedman, *The Secret Sayings of Jesus* (New York, 1960). R. McL. Wilson, *Studies in the Gospel of Thomas* (London, 1960). Ancient historians do not mention Jesus until very late. See J. G. Aufhauser, *Antike Jesuszeugnisse* (2d ed.; Berlin, 1925). W. de Boer, *Scriptorum Paganorum I-IV Saec. de Christianis Testimonia* (Leiden, 1948).

[3] See C. K. Barrett, *The Gospel according to St. John* (London, 1957) as well as the various Introductions to the New Testament.

40

Jesus' career means for the post-Easter church. Thus, for example, the feeding of the five thousand summons the church to no longer expect a miraculous bread supply, but to seek Jesus as the bread of life (Jn 6). John expresses all of this in a conceptual language different from the synoptics. He speaks, for example, not of "repentance," but of "being born again." This distinctive character of both the language and the manner of presentation prohibits any random mixture of synoptic and Johannine statements about Jesus. If we wish to use information from John's gospel about the earthly career of Jesus, we must skim off the kerygmatic expositions and go searching for the roots. This is only possible with assistance from the synoptic tradition. In our discussion we shall therefore concentrate on the synoptic tradition and then seek to make connections at crucial points with the Johannine presentation.

Even *in the synoptic gospels*, written thirty to fifty years after the close of Jesus' career, the picture of Jesus appears to be like a series of portraits painted one on top of the other. In order to find the original picture we must first of all try to skim off the layers that accrued during the transmission of the picture. As soon as we take a specific pericope or a specific question in Jesus' career and *compare the three evangelists with each other*, it becomes apparent that each evangelist selected and shaped the traditional material about Jesus differently depending upon his particular kerygmatic and theological intention and upon special traditions indigenous to him. By such comparison we can recognize variations in the traditional material about Jesus created by the editing of the evangelists and also by earlier transmitters. But just how much did accrue to the purely oral tradition in the thirty years before it was put down in writing? To answer this we must in the second place construct a picture of the rise and nature *of the gospel tradition*. It was not from a biographical and historical interest that the gospel tradition arose,[4] but rather from a concern to elucidate the Easter kerygma. The apostles proclaim Jesus' earthly career in order to show who the resurrected Lord is and how it came about that Israel rejected Him. The *Formgeschichte* viewpoint developed by M. Dibelius and R. Bultmann (1919 and 1921, respectively)[5] correctly saw that the gospel tradition originated in the kerygma and that it was shaped and transmitted as oral tradition. But the *Formgeschichte* viewpoint was in error when it thought that the *Sitz im Leben* of the gospel tradition was in congregational preaching, as though the gospel tradition was used to have Jesus give the young church particular counsel for particular congregational situations. From this viewpoint those things were ascribed to Jesus that were significant for the church and no distinction was made between the words of the earthly and the exalted Christ. So, for example, the pericope of plucking grain on the Sabbath was designed to have Jesus justify the young church's freedom from the Sabbath commandment. This presupposition of early *Formgeschichte* is simply not valid. In the entire preaching literature of primitive Christianity from the Pauline letters to 2 Clement we find, except for the paranesis, virtually no gospel tradition.

The epistles as preaching wish to proclaim what the exalted Lord has to say to His church. The gospel tradition, however, is concerned first and foremost with proclaiming who the exalted Lord is. Consequently the gospels are to be read initially as witness accounts of Jesus' earthly career and only secondarily as counsel for specific congregational

[4] For this reason it is impossible to write a "Leben Jesu," a biography of Jesus from the standpoint of a neutral observer. Cf. A. Schweitzer, *The Quest of the Historical Jesus* (New York, 1950, 1961). M. Dibelius, *From Tradition to Gospel* (New York, 1935).

[5] R. Bultmann, *The History of the Synoptic Tradition*, trans. from the 3d German ed. (London, 1963). Cf. V. Taylor, *The Formation of the Gospel Tradition* (London, 1933). B. Gerhardson, *Memory and Manuscript* (Upsala, 1961) introduces a new point of departure for investigating the history of traditions.

42

situations. Therefore in view of our knowledge of the congregational situation we are permitted at best only a very limited amount of skimming-off subsequent expansions of the original tradition. More important is, in the third place, the counter question: Which traditions prove to be original? To this question we can apply a negative and a positive criterion: (a) There are words and actions of Jesus that stand in bold contrast not only with His Jewish environment, but also with the life and thought of the primitive Christian church. So, for example, His statement against divorce. Even these few undoubtedly genuine traditions when properly understood yield a picture of Jesus' situation. (b) Additional portions prove to be genuine by virtue of their connection and congruity with Jesus' situation. Between the core tradition that this method yields and those later modifications that, on the other hand, can be skimmed off there remains a stratum the individual elements of which are uncertain. The total picture, however, is scarcely affected by this stratum.[6] In the following investigation we shall constantly be applying these principles, even if the actual analysis of a given tradition's history is not being overtly and expressly performed.[7]

[6] The fact that it is possible and necessary to develop a picture of Jesus' earthly career in this fashion can now be seen in the Bultmann school itself, viz., in G. Bornkamm's book (see note 1) and in the report by J. M. Robinson, A New Quest of the Historical Jesus (London, 1959). A cross-section of the current discussion is to be found in H. Ristow and K. Matthiae (eds.), Der historische Jesus und der kerygmatische Christus (2d ed.; Berlin, 1961).

[7] For a worthwhile confrontation with the issues raised by the history of traditions, see the introductions to the individual pericopes in V. Taylor, The Gospel according to St. Mark (4th ed.; London, 1957).

Chapter III

Jesus as God's Final Ambassador for All Israel

Together with other scholars Bultmann[8] concludes concerning Jesus' relationship to Judaism: "Jesus was not a 'Christian' but a Jew." There is no doubt that Jesus was, to His dying day, a member of the Jewish people and that He spoke and thought in their pattern of concepts and ideas. But what Bultmann's thesis really says is that Jesus did not Himself burst the framework of Judaism; that His expulsion from Judaism, like the killing of John the Baptist, was only the arbitrary act of a group within Judaism; and that when His followers later separated themselves from Judaism they did so on the basis of factors that were not originally present in the earthly ministry of Jesus.

This thesis agrees on all significant points with the opinion held by the majority of Jesus' Jewish contemporaries. Outwardly, Jesus gave the impression that he was a scribe who, accompanied by his circle of students, "taught" around the country (cf. Mk 1.22). However, judged by the content of his actions, he appeared to be more like a prophet, not one of the contemporary Zealot prophets but rather one in the tradition of the ancient prophets such as Elijah or John the Baptist. (Mk 6.14ff.; 8.28). A disinterested Jewish spectator would therefore have conceded that Jesus was largely without parallel in his own time, but still within the framework of Judaism, a prophet like John the Baptist.

This judgment, close as it is to Bultmann's thesis, appears at first to be confirmed by further investigation, but

---

8 *Das Urchristentum im Rahmen der antiken Religionen* (Zürich, 1949), p. 78; cf. *Existence and Faith* (New York, 1960), pp. 183-201.

in the final analysis it proves to be inadequate. The question of Jesus' relationship to Judaism must be based on the religious structure of Judaism and must be phrased thus: How did Jesus define His position toward the various movements in Judaism, and from which one did He Himself come?

1. *Jesus and the Religious Movements in Judaism*

In the gospels Jesus seems to be carrying on a running controversy with the Pharisees and their scribes. Other groups appear only very incidentally. Thus Jesus' controversy with Judaism, which largely determined His course of action, was carried on essentially as a *dispute with Pharisaism.*

Source criticism has raised an objection to this view, for it asserts that it was tradition which routinely inserted the word "Pharisees" for opponents of Jesus who are unnamed in the original sources. This is true in a few cases. But in the majority of instances the context verifies the authentic use of the word.

Moreover, the view that Jesus' controvesy with Judaism was essentially a conflict with Pharisaism was brought into disrepute by liberal theologians who, seeing it one-sidedly and distorted, proceeded to formulate a moralistic picture of Jesus as the champion of prophetic, independent ethical religiosity over against the dead ritualism of the Pharisees. In effect, they created a caricature of the Pharisees and then turned Jesus' message into a watered-down form of Pharisaism. In contrast to this moralistic modernism, research in the history of religions placed strong emphasis on the eschatological and apocalyptic sides of Jesus' message, but misunderstood it as mythological. The fact of the matter is that Jesus' work can be understood only when both sides are kept in focus. Only when one considers seriously the call to repentance that he addressed to the Pharisees does the message of the coming kingdom become clear, and vice

45

versa. Jesus' work was bipolar throughout, directed on the one hand toward God's already existent covenant with Israel under the Law, and on the other toward the coming kingdom. That is why His controversy with the Pharisees, who were the most energetic representatives of the Law, was a decisive part of His activity, and why the interpretation of this dispute is basic for understanding His work.

What was there in *Jesus' own background* that brought Him into conflict with the Pharisees? Until very recently, the explanation for this opposition was, so it was thought, to be found in some connection that He might have had with anti-Pharisaic movements in Palestinian Judaism.

The first explanation offered was the fact that Jesus came from Galilee where, because of the greater frequency of social relations between Jews and Gentiles, Judaism was supposedly more liberal than it was around Jerusalem. In view of the great mixtures of the people of Galilee, it has even been said that Jesus may not have been Jewish. These hypotheses simply do not stand up under historical investigation. The fact of the matter is that Galilean Judaism did not consist merely of a thin layer of colonists and others who had been brought there by the Maccabean conquest and who had had Judaism forced upon them. The Jews of Galilee were a permanent group that had lived there ever since the destruction of the Northern Kingdom and which, like the whole Diaspora, was completely in accord with Jerusalem in its allegiance to the Law. Galilee was, after all, the home of Zealotism. Differences there certainly were between the Judaism of Galilee and that of Jerusalem, and these differences may have had their effects on early Christianity, although perhaps not as significantly as Lohmeyer assumes; but they do not explain the conflict between Jesus and Pharisaism.[9]

Then it was maintained that Jesus was from the Ana-

[9] S. E. Johnson, *Jesus in His Homeland* (New York, 1957).

46

wim (the "down-and-outers") in the Am-ha-arez, or from the Enoch group in Galilee,[10] or from some third group that included both of these. But these hypotheses collapse on their own shaky historical foundations. Certain historians have spun stories about "the quiet ones in the land," supposedly Jews who had been left behind by the development of Judaism and who continued to practice the piety of the Psalter; actually, the only hint of their existence, that is, the canticles in early chapters of Luke, do not date back beyond early Christian times. As for Jesus' blessing of the poor in the Beatitudes, even its version in the "Ebionite" parts of St. Luke's special tradition does not suggest that it was directed to any particular religious or social class, least of all a circle of the Anawim. Rather, it was a call directed to all to repent.

The only one of these hypotheses that demands serious consideration is the suggestion of Jesus' connection with apocalyptic. Researchers in the history of religion since A. Schweitzer[11] have given an almost exclusive emphasis to apocalyptic as the background of Jesus' life and work. Now it is certainly true that Jesus very often used apocalyptic expressions. But neither from His own words nor from the bulk of New Testament literature can any literary connections be found with the post-canonical apocalyptic writings that are extant today, not even with the Enoch literature. If we want to see how an apocalyptic perspective would affect a document of primitive Christianity, we need only to look at Jude. Still less did Jesus actually adopt the specific apocalyptic world view as His own. Jesus' primary concern is that God's dominion be enacted in the present and

[10] R. Otto, *The Kingdom of God and the Son of Man* (Boston, 1951), pp. 13ff.

[11] *Op. cit.*, pp. 223ff. Currently the concern of a group of younger German theologians, for which see W. Pannenberg (ed.), *Offenbarung als Geschichte* (Göttingen, 1961). On the opposite side is W. D. Davies, *Christian Origins and Judaism* (Philadelphia, 1962), pp. 20-30.

not merely in the future, whereas for the apocalyptic writers the kingdom can come only via the destruction of the world. They seek to reckon when the kingdom will come, whereas Jesus dismisses any such calculations (Lk 17.20ff.).

The statements made by the New Testament itself, if looked at in terms of the history of religions, seem to direct our attention elsewhere in answering the question where Jesus came from. Before Jesus publicly appeared in Galilee, He was with John the Baptist at the Jordan and very likely also won some of His first disciples from the circle associated with John (Jn 1.35ff.; 3.22; 4.1). Of course John's own religious characteristics place him in the company of the Essenes and the Jewish Baptists. For this reason deism and early rationalism connected Jesus Himself with the Essenes.[12] When the DSS were discovered, many scholars thought that at Qumran the roots of Jesus and primitive Christianity had finally been discovered. Since then, however, scholars who still see large areas of affiliation between Jesus and the Essenes have expressed themselves more modestly about Jesus' actual dependence on them.[13] Serious scholarship today has come to the following conclusions: The DSS have illuminated our knowledge of the Jewish background to primitive Christianity in ways that were never anticipated. Thereby many of the statements of the New Testament are much more intelligible than before, since this segment of Judaism, too, is tied to primitive Christianity by all sorts of threads in the tradition. But the DSS discovery has not demolished the previously existing

[12] After the publication of the Mandaean texts there arose, around 1920, the conjecture that the label Nazarene applied to Jesus betrayed that he came from a Jewish Baptist sect of the Nazarenes which Epiphanius mentions. The conjecture proved to be baseless, however, when (1) it became evident that the Mandaeans themselves were not a pre-Christian phenomenon and (2) philological investigation showed that the title "Nazarene" simply meant a native or a resident of Jesus' home town (TWNT, IV, 879-884).

[13] E.g., A. Dupont-Sommer, The Essene Writings from Qumran (Oxford, 1961), pp. 373-378. M. Burrows (Chap. II, note 11), gives a good overview of the scholarly discussion.

picture of primitive Christianity and its Jewish background. With reference to Jesus Himself the facts of the matter are that His teaching has only formal association with Essene ethics and expectations of the end. He too radicalized the commandments and lived in imminent expectation. But the content of His teaching is illuminated more by its contrast than by its connection with Essene doctrine. His only personal resemblance to the "teacher of righteousness" was that He too claimed scriptural backing for his opposition to the prevalent tradition in Judaism and thus also came in conflict with its representative leaders. But Jesus did not gather unto Himself the true Israel as that teacher of the Law did. Instead He called all Israel to that divine salvation which comes through His person. If Jesus did receive any stimulation from Essene circles, it was far less significant than what he received from apocalyptic and Pharisaic sources.

These, in brief outline, are examples of the attempts that have been made to explain Jesus' life and work, including His conflict with the Pharisees, by identifying Him with some non-Pharisaic movement or option in the Judaism of His day. A critical examination of these attempts serves only to confirm the explicit statements of the gospels that *Jesus gathered His disciples* not from any one particular movement but rather from the whole breadth of Judaism. Zealot and tax collector stood side by side in the circle of the twelve. Extremes that stagger the imagination were welded together in the creation of something new. As a result, primitive Christianity was to reflect in its own nature and structure the whole breadth of Judaism.

There is no convincing evidence that Jesus himself stemmed from any movement within the Judaism of His day. It was in controversy with the Pharisees, it is true, that His position in relation to Judaism came into focus; but this was because for Him Pharisaism was the only seriously debatable direction Judaism had taken—not because He had

49

associated Himself with some anti-Pharisee movement. Jesus took the Pharisees seriously. And the Pharisees took Him seriously.

When Jesus' contemporaries tried to fit Him into one of the Jewish movements of His day, they found, strange as it may seem, that His position was closest to that of the Pharisees. The gospels report only one dispute between Jesus and the *Sadducees* (Mk 12.18-27). This conversation was enough to prove that serious conversation between them was impossible. On this occasion, the Sadducees tried to foist off on Jesus the Pharisaic doctrine of resurrection, by implication suggesting that Jesus was practically a Pharisee. And then they tried to show how the Law itself made the Pharisees' doctrine of the resurrection look ridiculous. Jesus' reply exposed the poverty of their concept of God and the superficiality of their understanding of the scriptures. Jesus simply could not take the Sadducees seriously as representatives of a people under law and promise.

While the Sadducees took Jesus for some sort of Pharisee, the Pharisees suspected Him of *Zealotism* (Mk 12.13-17). But Jesus' answer to the question about giving tribute to Caesar sets him in bold contrast to Zealotism because of His command to render unto God the things that are God's, that is, everything.

Jesus and the Pharisees took each other seriously because they both took the Law seriously as God's commandment. For Jesus, the Pharisees and their scribes were the representatives of the Judaism of His time: The Pharisees as the best models of obedience to the Law, their scribes as the best administrators of the Law in Israel (Mk 12.32ff.).

Jesus' *attitude toward John the Baptist*[14] best illustrates what it was in His position that brought Him into conflict with the Pharisees. John was the only person in Judaism whom Jesus acknowledged as His forerunner (Mt 11.7-19).

[14] C. H. Kraeling, *John the Baptist* (New York, 1951). J. A. T. Robinson, "Elijah, John and Jesus," *NTS*, IV (1957/58), 263-81.

John demanded from all a once-and-for-all-time complete repentance. That was the only escape in the face of imminent judgment. By contrast the Pharisees preached a daily repentance, that is, a daily enacted contrition for individual transgressions of the commandments. The Essenes too required a once-and-for-all-time radical repentance, but for them it consisted in joining the sectarian community and submitting to the system of ritual and obedience to the Law. John baptized all those who wanted to repent with his unique and nonrepeatable baptism as a preliminary sign of the prophesied final purification (Ezek 36.25ff.; Mt 3.11 f.). Historically viewed, John belongs in the company of the Jewish Baptist movement. After his death he was adopted by this movement and even honored as a messianic prophet by one of the Baptist sects (Jn 120f.). But seen in the light of New Testament knowledge of God, John stood confronting Israel in the loneliness of an Old Testament prophet, an erratic "odd ball" to his contemporaries. Jesus' connection with John was not a matter of His becoming one of John's disciples, but He accepted John's call to repentance as God's call and requested John's baptism.

By submitting to the ministry of John the Baptist, Jesus obediently and therefore authoritatively latched on to the very heart of the revelation to which the scriptures testify. It was the preservation of this revelation—and also its violation—that had made Judaism what it was. Jesus' firm attachment to that revelation undergirded all of His teaching, even though the form of His exegesis was traditionally Jewish. As far as content goes Jesus' understanding of scripture was actually not less independent on the Jewish exegetical tradition than was that of Qumran's "teacher of righteousness."

An examination of the relationship of Jesus to the movements within Judaism therefore confirms the thesis proposed by such historical scholars as Bultmann that Jesus renewed the protest of the Old Testament prophets against a Judaism which had usurped the Old Testament revelation; and confirms that Jesus, like John the Baptist, stood as an eschatological prophet within Judaism. To evaluate this thesis, we must first ask: Is or is not Jesus "more" than John the Baptist? Is He merely an authoritative mediator of God's final word, or does His word, as the Gospel According to St. John asserts, finally bear witness to Himself as the saving mediator? We can get a preliminary answer to this question by examining His absolutely unique position toward Israel as a whole.

2. Jesus and Israel

In His relation to the Jewish people as a whole, Jesus was basically different from any scribal representative of any of the Jewish movements, even from any prophet. Unlike the representatives of the various Jewish movements Jesus did not try to cull out of the "lost" multitude" a fellowship of the "true Israel" that by living according to His rules would receive the coming salvation. The circle of the twelve was no sect but rather a group of pupils, called to witness and to give an advance demonstration of a future fellowship that had nothing to do with a separate synagogue. Nowhere can we see signs of any other kind of organization among Jesus' disciples during His days on earth.[15]

Like John the Baptist and the prophets who went before him, Jesus called the entire people to repent because the eschaton was imminent. For Him the eschaton was God's coming salutary dominion of the end-time that would eradicate all wickedness and remove all evil (Mt 5.3-10). Even the most righteous, Jesus insisted, needed complete repentance; but at the same time the most desperately lost was called to this salvation—simply because he too was a child of Abraham (Lk 13.16; 19.9). Jesus saw the

[15] The circle of the 70 or 72 mentioned only in Lk 10.1 and 17 is most likely not historical.

52

whole Jewish people as the real Israel, God's people. Thus while He could grant that the Pharisees were the religious representatives of the people, He could not admit their claim to being the true Israel. Unlike John the Baptist, however, Jesus was not merely a preacher of repentance—not even of a repentance freed from legalistic casuistry and motivated by the imminence of the final eschaton. His encounter with Israel was not merely a controversy about a message; it was the making of salvation for the many. This is demonstrated first of all by the peculiar *concentration of His activity on the Jewish people*, in strict *distinction from Gentiles.*

All four gospels agree that Jesus' work on earth took place essentially among the Jews in Palestine. Contacts with non-Jews during His journey through Samaria or on His side-trips north and east of Galilee seem to have been, even according to John's gospel, the exceptions that prove the rule. None of His side-trips into non-Jewish country ever suggested an attempt to transfer His activity there (Jn 7.35). The final goal of Jesus' whole course of action was always and only Jerusalem, "the city of the great King" (Mt 5.35), the city of Judaism.

The isolated comments, usually unemphasized and incidental, in all four gospels attest to limitations placed on Jesus' activity. This reflects *Jesus' own intention.* He Himself observed the directive that He gave his apostles when He sent them out during His time on earth: "Go nowhere among the Gentiles, and enter no town of the Samaritans, but go rather to the lost sheep of the house of Israel" (Mt 10.5). In His meeting with the *Syrophoenician woman* He applied this same principle when He said: "It is not right to take the children's bread and throw it to the dogs" (Mk 7.27 par. Mt). What He meant was that a wholesale expansion of His activity to include the Gentiles would rob the Jewish people of what was rightfully theirs. This answer —painfully sharp as it seems to us—is not a reflection of the

53

narrowness of Talmudic Judaism, which jealously tried to restrict God's grace and truth to Israel; after all, this attitude dates only from the year 70. In Jesus' day even a Pharisaic rabbi would have been only too glad to listen to the request of this heathen woman in hope of making a proselyte (Mt 23.15). In this story, therefore, we see Jesus denying what a rabbi or even a prophet like Elijah would have granted. So we must understand Jesus' answer as an expression of the way He defined His unique mission of salvation. The miracles of help and healing that He performed were the fulfillment of the promise of salvation (Mt 11.4f. par. Lk), signs of the dawn of that final revelation of salvation which was to call Israel to repentance (Mt 11.20-24 par. Lk). As the agent of this new work of God, He was God's last messenger sent to the people entrusted with God's vineyard; He was to straighten out the relation between the tenants and their Lord (Mk 12.1-12 par.).[16] That is why He could not turn to the cities of the Gentiles when Israel rejected Him, even though He might have found more faith there (Mt 11.20ff. par. Lk). Instead, He had to hold out to the very end in Israel; and finally, in Jerusalem, He had to force the Jewish leaders to come to a decision about Him. In view of what sort of "generation" they were, this decision could only be to reject Him (Mt 23.29-39 par. Lk). Not until His death did His mission to Israel end.

It is therefore an inaccurate shifting of Jesus' original position when Mark inserts (7.27): "Let the children first be fed"; and when Luke (4.23-27) describes Jesus' work on earth from the same point of view. Both of these references read back into Jesus' work on earth the principle which was to apply only to the proclamation after His resurrection: "first the Jews, then the Gentiles" (Rom 1.16; Acts 13.46; et al.). Matthew, at least, states it correctly: in His days

[16] See the comment on this pericope in J. Jeremias, *The Parables of Jesus* (London, 1954) and C. H. Dodd, *The Parables of the Kingdom* (rev. ed.; London, 1936).

on earth, Jesus was "sent only to the lost sheep of the house of Israel" (Mt 15.24; cf. 10.5). But while Luke and Mark overlooked this principle, *John* grasped its full implication (Jn 12.20-24). When the Greeks asked to see Jesus, he replied: The grain of wheat must first die in the earth. Only after it has died can it bring forth much fruit.

This does not mean that salvation could not be offered to the "many," that is, to mankind, until some prior claim of the Jewish people had been satisfied. Rather, it means that the offer of salvation had to await the fulfillment of God's covenant with Israel (cf. Mk 10.45 par. Mt; Mk 14.24 par.). Jesus saw the Jewish people as "Israel," God's people, not because the Jews had in any way earned that title but simply because they were God's "vineyard," that is, under God's covenant they had been granted God's own life. It was on the basis of God's already existing ordinances of law and promise that Jesus, God's last messenger, called Israel to "render unto God the things that are God's." But this call to "turn back" was issued as a call to a new relationship with God, a relationship that Jesus Himself effected finally and completely by His death (Mk 14.24 par.). Thus, to state a preliminary conclusion, we may say that Jesus was not merely another John the Baptist. And therefore His encounter with Israel was not merely a controversy about a message. It was the making of salvation for the "many." Since Jesus saw Himself sent to Israel as a whole, His work of salvation began with those who were most wholly lost, and His call to repentance began with the Pharisees. His goal was not to reach everyone through the whole length and breadth of Judaism, including the Diaspora, but rather to confront the real representatives of Israel, the first as well as the last.

We have now sketched in broad outlines Jesus' encounter with Judaism. To fill in the details, we shall have to look at His controversy with the Pharisees.

Chapter IV

Jesus' Controversy with Pharisaism

1. The Course of the Controversy

The gospels do not all use the term "Pharisees" in the same way. Although the term is sometimes inserted in the text to designate opponents of Jesus who were unnamed in the sources, this is not particularly significant.[1] What is significant is its use in combination with the word "scribes" to give us that unrealistic formulation used only by Matthew and Luke, "the scribes and Pharisees." This blurring of a distinction is partially explained by the widening time gap between the original events and the documents reporting them. But in Matthew, at least, the phrase rests on a kernel of truth. Only those scribes who represented the Pharisaic movement were important in the controversy with Jesus. By the same token, mentioning the scribes along with the Pharisees emphasized that Jesus turned not only against the practice of the Pharisees but also against the doctrinal system that their scribes represented.

Jesus' opponents are invariably referred to not as individual persons but as the proponents of one of the particular movements within Judaism. Thus, the normal generalized designation, "the Pharisees," expresses a basic fact of this controversy. What mattered was not this or that individual but rather man under the Law. The united front that opposed Jesus was not united around an organization but around a cause; whoever stood with the Pharisees would inevitably have to reject Jesus and inevitably fall under His criticism.

The controversy between Jesus and His opponents

<hr>

[1] E.g., Mt 3.7; 12.38,41 where par. Lk reads "others," Mt 22.34,41 where par. Mk reads "the scribes."

erupted partly because Jesus concentrated directly on the Pharisees with His call to repentance and partly because the Pharisees protested that with His redemptive work Jesus was abolishing the Law. The former is Matthew's premise, the latter Mark's and Luke's.

Matthew develops Jesus' entire proclamation as a condemnation of Pharisaism. He pictures Jesus and the Pharisees as always irreconcilably on opposite sides. (John carries this view to its ultimate conclusion.) Matthew begins with the blessing of the poor in spirit and the demand for a righteousness that "exceeds that of the scribes and Pharisees" (Mt 5.20) and concludes Jesus' public preaching with His great indictment against them (Mt 23). Luke, on the other hand, pictures Jesus' redemptive work not only as a scandal to the self-righteous but also as a saving call to them to repent. Therefore he also records Jesus' sitting at table with the Pharisees (Lk 7.36; 11.37; 14.1) and even being earnestly questioned by them (Lk 13.31; 17.20; cf. Mk 12.28). Mark relates the controversy, although without strong emphasis, as a protest on the part of the Pharisees against Jesus' saving work and His interpretation of the Law (Mk 2f.; 7.1-13), and for him the controversy ends with Jesus warning His disciples to beware of the Pharisees (Mk 12.37b-40).

Historically, both of these points of view, which tend to exclude each other in the evangelists' presentations, were most likely intermingled constantly. We shall begin our more detailed analysis by looking at Jesus' condemning call to the Pharisees to repentance based on the Law, and then we shall examine the foundation of that call in the saving call to repentance based on His saving work.

2. The Indictment Against the Pharisees and the Scribes

The condemning call to repentance that Jesus directed to the Pharisees and to the scribes is stated as a series of "woes" in Lk 11.39-51 par. Mt 23.1-36; Mk 12.37b-40 par. Lk; Mk 8.15 par.; in Lk 11 the woes are properly applied to both. Here Jesus, as the last of the prophets, was calling negligent tenants back to God's commandment (Mt 23.29-36 par. Lk). He was addressing the representatives of Israel who had cut themselves and others off from saving fellowship with God (Mt 23.13-15 par. Lk 11.52). This message, based on the commandments, was a necessarily condemning call to repentance. It was that woe upon self-righteousness which in Matthew's view was the direct opposite of that saving call to repentance expressed in the Beatitudes in Mt 5, the blessing of the poor by virtue of the coming kingdom. The indictment against the Pharisees and scribes as it was summed up by the Evangelists read: "hypocrisy." In them appearance and reality contradicted each other. The scribes taught God's commandment and the Pharisees zealously tried to put it into practice, but neither obeyed it. What was their disobedience? Jesus did not contest the factual validity of the Pharisees' boasting (Lk 18.11f.; cf. Mk 10.20); but He did make clear that this legalistic idea of fulfilling the Law by doing the works that it commanded was a far cry from what the Law actually demands, especially from that attitude of heart that the Law demands (Lk 11.39-44 par. Mt). And He further insisted that this disobedience of the heart was encouraged rather than exposed by their niggling over fine questions of right and wrong, that it was camouflaged rather than remedied by their zeal. The scribes, in their exegesis of the Law, were concerned to determine its boundaries precisely so as to minimize the risk of violating it. But in actuality this helped them to evade it (Mk 7.9-13 par. Mt). The Pharisees, by constantly harping on the smallest points of the Law, hid from themselves and others their violations of the chief commandments, those of justice and mercy and faith (Mt 23.23 par. Lk; Mt 23.25f.). In the last analysis, it was the very thing that constituted the honor of the scribes and the righteousness of the Pharisees which made it possible for them to disobey. And thus was unmasked that real defect which turned everything that the scribes and Pharisees did into a fearful record of total disobedience: *they used God's commandments to elevate themselves.* The scribes interpreted the commandments, and the Pharisees tried their best to keep them, not for the sake of God's glory but their own (Mk 12.38f.; Mt 6.1-18; 23.5). This was not merely some deficiency in their moral thinking; this was original sin. And so the hypocrisy of which Jesus accused the scribes and the Pharisees as representatives of the Law was not merely a discrepancy between teaching and practice or between legalism and moral concern—although this was a fault of Pharisaism just as it is, more or less, a fault of every idealistic moralism; but the Pharisaic hypocrisy was something more —an elemental rebelliousness that flares up when it encounters God's own Law. To clarify this we must now address ourselves to the question that arises: Is not this harsh judgment contradicted by the willingness the scribes and Pharisees so often evidenced to sacrifice for the Law and to defend it? *Jesus' judgment was not analytic but synthetic,* that is, not an analysis of individual cases but rather a synthesis of the whole matter. This judgment uncovered a fact not generally known: The scribes and Pharisees were not only different from what they wanted to *appear* to be but also from what they wanted to *be.* It was a prophetic judgment upon man under the Law substantiated by that man's inevitable reaction to Jesus' work. It was in this vein that Paul definitively amplified this judgment from the point of view of the cross in Rom 7.15-25. We shall now examine this inevitable reaction of the Pharisees to Jesus' work.

3. *The New Commandment and Pharisaism*

Jesus became the offense and the ruination of Pharisaic legalism. His own free actions and those of His disciples were the signs of His break with it. They demonstrated this freedom of action especially in their *attitude toward the Sabbath commandment*—a particularly good commandment for them to use since it was a central and sacrosanct one throughout all of Judaism that could not be broken without people knowing about it.

In exercising this freedom Jesus made clear first of all His *rejection of the scribes' interpretation of the Law* ("the tradition of the elders," the Halacha) that for the Pharisees was the binding rule of their conduct, the verbal Torah (Mk 7.5). Jesus based this rejection both on the commandment of the Old Testament and on His saving work. The tradition, Jesus insisted, actually encouraged men to evade God's commandments. One example, Mk 7.10-13 par. Mt, serves as an instance to call the whole system to judgment (Mk 7.6-9 par. Mt). The full hypocrisy of the tradition was exposed when Jesus' enemies used it to condemn His healing of the sick on the Sabbath day: lawful indeed it was to help an animal on the Sabbath—but not a human being! (Lk 12.15f.; 14.5f.). Notice that in this case Jesus made no attempt to justify His course of action by the casuistry of the scribes; rather He sought to show up the questionable nature of all scribal casuistry. The tradition was simply hypocrisy for it was not based, as claimed, on God's will, but rather on an attempt—conscious or unconscious—to delimit the scribes' own obligations. Because this scribal interpretation of the Law and the corresponding practice of the Pharisees misused the commandments by making them means of self-assertion before God and man, Jesus shoved this interpretation aside and brought man face to face with God's commandments themselves.

Not only that, but Jesus also withdrew the Old Testament commandments themselves as a support for this legalism. He justified His healing on the Sabbath with the question (Mk 3.4 par. Lk): "Is it lawful on the Sabbath to do good or to do harm, to save life or to kill?" Jesus' alternative question exploded the idea of the Sabbath law as an absolutely binding regulation, for certainly it has no absolute hold any more if this inclusive, far-reaching alternative applied: to save life, which is the fundamental work of God Himself, is good; to destroy life, which is the work of Satan (cf. Jn 8.44), is evil. Such a demand encompasses every bit of man's life. It is as all-inclusive as the commandments of the Sermon on the Mount (Mt 5.21-48) or the statement in Mk 12:17: "Render to God the things that are God's"—that is to say, everything. Jewish scholars to this day raise the objection that these total commandments are ideal but incapable of fulfillment, that they are fanatically super-spiritualistic whereas the Law itself is realistic. As a matter of fact, is there really any human course of action that concretely and constantly performs God's work by preserving life? Jesus makes the claim that this work of God does occur through Him, for He follows up His own spoken word with the demonstrative healing of the sick. It is at this very point that all interpretations of Jesus' position toward Pharisaic legalism which are nonchristological— that is, which do not take Jesus' own person into account— fail completely and degenerate to some kind of naive moralism.

The *hidden meaning of Jesus' attitude toward the Sabbath* becomes apparent in the story of the disciples plucking grain (Mk 2.23-28 par.). Because of this behavior of His disciples Jesus is called to account by the Pharisees since according to Oriental notions still valid today the teacher is responsible for the actions of his disciples. In His reply Jesus does not actually justify the disciples' behavior. Instead He justifies His having given them the permission. He does this by means of two typological deductions from scripture. If David was permitted to break the Law by virtue of his special calling, then all the more does Jesus have analogous permission. He may allow those who have answered His call by giving up everything and following Him to infringe on the commandment of rest in quieting their hunger by plucking grain. If the priests are allowed to infringe on the commandment of rest for the sake of the Temple, then all the more is this permissible for Jesus' own sake, since Jesus is "greater than the Temple," just as He is greater than David (Mt 12.6). Of course such a "greater one" can only be the "promised One." Thus Jesus is here giving a veiled messianic justification of His actions.

There is on the other hand a statement found only in Mark's transmission that seems to justify a very generalized attitude of freedom toward the Sabbath. "The Sabbath was made for man, not man for the Sabbath" (Mk 2.27). Some exegetes hold that this justification of Sabbath-freedom is so different from those represented in the grain-plucking pericope that it alone genuinely comes from Jesus. They reason that Jesus simply proclaimed a generalized freedom toward the Sabbath and that the primitive church tied this freedom to Jesus' person. However, such an explanation misunderstands this statement of Jesus. Jesus' statement is reminiscent of a doctrinal thesis of the Rabbis: "The Sabbath is committed to you; not: you are committed to the Sabbath." With this thesis the Rabbis justified helping a man in mortal danger even if this infringed on the Sabbath rest. Jesus' statement is not intended to outdo the Rabbis in liberalizing the Sabbath. He does not want to say that fallen man can administer the Sabbath according to his own needs. Instead He calls to mind, as He also did about marriage (Mk 10.6ff.), the original intention of the Creator, namely, because man is God's creature he may make free use of the Sabbath as of every gift of God (cf. Gen 1.28). But according to Jesus, God's man is only that man who obeys His total demand, that is, Jesus Himself and all who follow Him. Consequently Mark is absolutely right when he draws from this statement the conclusion, "so the Son of Man is lord even of the Sabbath" (Mk 2.28). According to Jesus, "the Son of Man," by virtue of Dan

7.13, is that man who himself completely belongs to God's world and brings God's end-time dominion, namely, Jesus Himself. However, in Aramaic "son of man" means simply "a man" and therefore many exegetes even to this day think this statement originally referred merely to mankind in general. Here too the messianic significance is veiled.

Thus we see that Jesus actually repealed the Sabbath commandment with a bipolar replacement, first, a new and total demand and, second, a new fulfillment of God's will which He Himself initially achieved. Jesus' attitude was not a universally valid regulation for new Sabbath behavior, but a *demand for a definite attitude toward His own person*. The Pharisees met this demand by deciding to kill Him precisely because of His attitude toward the Sabbath (Mk 3.6 par.).

In John's gospel we find a definitive exposition of what the Sabbath controversy was really all about, and in the light of that exposition the meaning of the synoptics becomes clear. First of all, as to the circumstances, it is clear from both Sabbath stories (Jn 5.1-18; 7.21-24; 9.1-41) that the Sabbath commandment was unquestionably broken (Jn 5.10; 9.14). Jesus' justification for breaking it is equally clear: "My Father is working still, and I am working" (Jn 5.17). That is to say, the Sabbath was broken by the saving and life-giving work of God. And "this was why the Jews sought all the more to kill him, because he not only broke the sabbath but also called God his Father, making himself equal with God" (Jn 5.18; cf. 19.7). Here we have a clear statement of the presupposition behind Mk 3.6 par. Jesus seemed to them to be worthy of death not because He had committed what was actually a minor breach of the Sabbath—after all, the "sinners" were certainly guilty of much more serious violations—but because *He defended His lawbreaking as a fulfillment of the will of God*. That meant the end of the absolute validity of the Law. And that, in turn, meant the end of Judaism. If *Judaism* wanted to remain what it was it *had to reject Jesus.* The attitude of Judaism toward Jesus did not grow out of any explicit claims on His part of being the Messiah but out of His attitude toward the Law and His defense of this attitude.

What was the hidden meaning behind *Jesus' attitude toward the Law*—the meaning hidden at least from Judaism? Jesus does not dismiss the Law as an antiquated stage of religious development nor as a phase in redemptive history that had run its course. "Until heaven and earth pass away, not an iota, not a dot, will pass from the law until all is accomplished" (Mt 5.18 par. Lk). This statement records accurately Jesus' evaluation of the Law, by which term He always meant the Mosaic law of the Old Testament. The validity of the Law is limited by this double "until." On the one hand the Law is valid until the end of this world, in contrast to Jesus' words that are valid even when "heaven and earth shall pass away" (Mk 13.31 par.). On the other hand it is valid until the end-time fulfillment occurs. This fulfillment, however, would not first occur in the new world, but already now through Jesus Himself (Mt 5.17). Consequently Jesus always took for granted that in this world the Law with its commandments and its structure of retribution (Ex 19.5; 20.5) continues to remain valid (Mk 10.17ff. par.; 12.28ff. par.). But from this basic presupposition on the Law He then proceeded to call people into a new situation that, as was pointedly spelled out in the pericope of the rich young man, consists in the challenging demand to follow Him.

What does this new situation have to do with the *commandments of the Law?* Interpreters have said that Jesus emphasized the permanence of natural law above the restricted validity of ceremonial law; that He called for a genuine ethical concern in place of casuistry; that He summarized all of the commandments in the commandment of love; that He demanded "genuine, radical obedience in place of both ritualistic piety and a legal understanding of man's relationship with God" (Bultmann). Each of these interpretations fastens too exclusively upon some one aspect of what Jesus was driving at. His concern itself was strictly God-centered (on a hidden christological basis). Man has perverted the Old Testament commandments, making of them a rule that he could not only master but could then use as protection against God's claim upon him. Jesus welded the commandments to God's total and absolute demands, the demands of God the creator and perfector (Mt 19.4ff., 12) (this is the theocentric emphasis); and He did so as the one through whom God was establishing His dominion (this is the christological basis). Consequently all of Jesus' other statements concerning Old Testament commandments and Pharisaic casuistry run along essentially the same lines as those cited in connection with the Sabbath commandment, whether these other statements involved His attitude toward the laws of cleanliness and Temple service, or toward the Ten Commandments, or even toward the Old Testament commandment of love.[2] Consequently Jesus never set down any systematic rules about the continued validity of Old Testament Law or indeed about any new Law but rather used individual Old Testament commandments as examples to articulate the one overriding demand for total obedience. The more this total obedience is bound directly by God's will, the more it transcends the laws that regulate human life on this earth. This direct bond with God's will gives this obedience definite content. This new bond with God coupled with freedom from the Law and from the world is received by being bound to Jesus' saving work that annuls the salutary order of the Law. Put another way, man receives this bond by receiving Jesus' forgiveness.

[2] Mk 7.14f.; 11.15ff.; Mt 5.21f., 27f., 33-37; Lk 10.25-37.

4. Jesus' Forgiveness and Pharisaism

Just as the Pharisees had to regard Jesus' radical demand as an attack on the absolute validity of the Law, so they had to regard Jesus' forgiveness as a blasphemous disintegration of the Law's own way of salvation.

Jesus associated with sinners in a way that defied the principle of Pharisaism—which was, remember, the principle of Judaism as a whole. He entered the houses of sinners and ate with them. This signified the closest fellowship. This kind of behavior brought protests not only from the Pharisees (Mk 2.16 par.; Lk 7:39) but also from the people (Lk 19.7). The danger in associating thus with people who despised the Law was not only ritualistic uncleanness (which Peter avoided even years after Pentecost, Gal 2.12f.); it also involved a disregard for sin and a temptation against which the first Psalm warns: "Blessed is the man who walks not in the counsel of the wicked . . . nor sits in the seat of scoffers."

Jesus admitted that there was some justice in this protest when He said (Mk 2.17 par.): "Those who are well have no need of a physician, but those who are sick." Acknowledging the law's own salutary order ("this do and thou shalt live"), *Jesus took seriously the Jewish distinction between "sinners" and "righteous."* A "sinner" was one who actually disregarded God's Law;[3] a "righteous" man was one who seriously sought to fulfill the Law. In normal daily life it was not difficult to tell one from the other. Jesus also viewed these sinners as "sick" people; and the fellowship He gave them was not that of an accomplice in crime but of a physician.

[3] "Sinners" are, e.g., "the Gentiles" (Mt 5.47 par. Lk 6.33) or within Israel "the tax collectors" (Mk 2.15 par.; Mt 5.46 par. Lk 6.32; Mt. 11.19 par.; Lk 18.13; 19.7). For the Essenes and even for the Pharisees everyone who does not belong to their group is essentially "a sinner." Jesus uses the term, however, with the generally accepted meaning developed in the Psalms, and then expresses the burden of His specific message with certain clearly unambiguous examples.

The parable of the prodigal son in Lk 15 illustrates in what manner Jesus was *the sinner's physician*. This parable is not, as liberalism would have it, an illustration of the fatherly love of God; nor is it, as Bultmann maintains, an authoritarian proclamation of God's love toward sinners. Rather, as the introduction to the parable makes clear (Lk 15.1f.), it is an illustration of what happens when Jesus grants His fellowship to sinners. Acceptance into fellowship with Jesus means acceptance into fellowship with God. An inevitable consequence of this is a return to obedience as the stories of Zacchaeus (Lk 19.8) and the sinful woman (Lk 7.45ff.) make clear. Only in very rare cases was this forgiveness that Jesus granted through His helping fellowship expressly spoken to a person (Mk 2.5 par.; Lk 7.47-49).

This explanation of Jesus' fellowship with sinners was a scandal to the Pharisees, the righteous. At the same time, it was the final inviting call to them to repent. The nature of their sin and the way to escape from it were definitively portrayed in the case of the *older brother of the prodigal son*.

What Jesus had to say about this older brother is that he was guilty, even in the eyes of the Law. Note Lk 15.29: "Lo, these many years I have served you and I never disobeyed your command; yet you never gave me a kid that I might make merry with my friends." Here we have the most graphic picture of Pharisaic piety imaginable. This is man under the Law! He does indeed keep God's commandments outwardly (Lk 18.10-12; Mk 10.20). But he does so as a slave obeys his master—not out of love but for the sake of reward. And what a reward! Just to make merry with his friends! Is there any difference between the ambition of the older brother and that of his younger brother? Granted that the younger brother attempted to achieve it by the wrong means while the older brother played it straight. But is there any real difference of intent? And now notice Lk 15.31, where the father says: "Son, you are always with me, and all that is mine is yours." What Jesus is saying here is that the proper joy and reward of a son is being with the father. It was a mark of slavishness in the older brother to be hankering for a kid so that he could make merry with friends. The Pharisee, in other words, did not love God, and therefore he could not love his brother. He used his sinful brother only as a dark backdrop against which to display his own comparative righteousness (Lk 15.30; 18.11). The Law itself first exposed this sinful chink in the armor of self-righteousness. But the chink opened into a great, gaping hole when confronted with the saving work of Jesus.

Since the righteous brother wanted to be rewarded for his accomplishments, he was naturally angry at his father's goodness toward the prodigal (Lk 15.28; Mt 20.15). In just the same way, the completely egocentric, slavish attitude of the righteous Pharisees toward God and their loveless-ness toward their neighbors became glaringly evident when they protested against Jesus' saving of sinners. In their at-titude the Pharisees took a position at the opposite pole from the God who desires "mercy and not sacrifice."[4] And thus, while the sin of these righteous ones was not as obvious as that of the sinners, it went infinitely deeper. For not only did they sin against the Law; they sinned with the help of the Law.

In the parable, Jesus called the Pharisee out of the fields in which he had been working as a slave and invited him into the father's house, into the fellowship of saved sinners (Lk 15.32). For the righteous, repentance means entering into the joy of the saved and rejoicing that they are the saved. It means giving up all boasting about ac-complishments and reward. It means getting rid of this slavish attitude toward God. It means hungering and thirst-ing for the fellowship which the father gives as a free gift

[4] With this citation from Hos 6.6 Matthew explains very strikingly the sense in which Jesus and the Pharisees understood the Law differently (Mt 9.13; 12.7).

of mercy, and it means loving the sinful brother with forgiveness.

Thus the final invitation of Jesus to the righteous is
found in His conduct toward the sinners. The parables in
Lk 15 and in Lk 7.40-47 and 18.9 are *invitations to the
righteous*—invitations which, oddly enough, always take the
form of a call to come and *join the saved sinners.* This was
the way Jesus actually worked—beginning with the last, as
the parable of the vineyard illustrates (Mt 20.8), and finally
offering to the first what the last had already received.
Notice that Jesus did not turn to the sinners as a kind of
last resort after others had refused Him. No, He actually
began with them.[5] "I came not to call the righteous, but
sinners" (Mk 2.17 par.; cf. Lk 19.10). With God there is
"more joy . . . over one sinner who repents than over ninety-
nine righteous persons who need no repentance"[6] (Lk 15.3-
10). God's plan of salvation did not merely envision a salvation, as the Old Testament emphasized, that sinners
might *also* share; it provided for a salvation that sinners
would receive *before* the righteous were called home. This
is good news! This is gospel! This was the end of Pharisaism, the end of all boasting (Rom 3.27), the dawn of
salvation *sola gratia*, the opening of a new way to the throne
of God, the new way of salvation!

In its response to this invitation Pharisaism showed its
true colors. As it turned out, the long path of the prodigal

[5] The parable of the marriage feast (Mt 22.1-4 par. Lk) is not a
description of Jesus' missionary methods, but a warning interpretation of
Israel's rejecting him. Those who were initially invited are Israel. The
beggars are the Gentiles! The parable belongs in the same category with
such pericopes as Mt 8.11f.; 11.16-24. Jesus purposefully does not come
first of all, as the Pharisees expect, to the righteous! The evangelists
Matthew and Luke have accurately grasped the central meaning of the
original parable, but then, each in his own way, they have interwoven the
church's subsequent missionary experience with Israel.

[6] To say that the righteous "need no repentance" (Lk 15.7) or
"have no need of a physician" (Mk 2.17 par.) is to make a rhetorical
assertion. What sort of repentance the righteous really need becomes apparent in the brother of the prodigal son!

son back from the far country to his father's house proved easier than the older brother's short step in from the field of slavish service. The sinner need only leave his filth behind; the righteous must also leave his righteousness. It was not so difficult for Levi and Zacchaeus to give up the property they had dishonestly acquired as it was for the rich young man to give up possessions that were his by every legal right. And so we get the situation described in the parable of the dissimilar sons (Mt 21.28-32): the righteous say "yes" to God's will but do not fulfill it; the tax collectors and sinners say "no" and then fulfill His will anyway. And so "the tax collectors and the harlots go into the kingdom of God before you," that is, you, the righteous, do not go in at all (Mt 21.31).

Because the Pharisees did not accept Jesus' invitation they continued to regard Him as a blasphemer who was trying to destroy God's law—a blasphemer who had to be removed from Judaism.

5. *Summary Evaluation of Jesus' Attitude Toward the Law*

Any evaluation of Jesus Himself, His purpose, or His relationship to Judaism depends even today on how one interprets Jesus' attitude toward the Law. The method of comparative religion seems to commend itself in comparing Jesus' attitude with those views current in His Jewish environment. This comparison reveals, for example, under Bultmann's hand, a two-fold radicalization. Jesus radicalized both the demand of God and His forgiveness, the latter being also a part of Pharisee theology.[7] This radicalizing is eschatological, that is, it is in accordance with Jesus' an-

[7] The Rabbis taught that whoever repented of his transgression against the commandments with active contrition would be forgiven through God's goodness. They therefore urged daily contrition and repentance. Grave sins, however, were not removed until atonement was made by the annual Day of Atonement or by death. *Billerbeck*, I, 169. E. Sjöberg, *Gott und die Sünder im palästinensischen Judentum* (Stuttgart, 1939), pp. 125-83, 212-22. Moore, (Chap. II, note 8) I, 497-545.

nouncement that the end-time dominion of God, a new world, is due to burst forth at any moment. Since the discovery of the *DSS* we now know that both of these characteristics also typify the Essenes' view of the Law. This has led one of Bultmann's pupils to compare this "late Jewish heretical radicalism" with that of Jesus.[8] His thorough statistical investigation reveals that in Jesus' view God's demand is more radical and man is more totally dependent on God's grace than is the case with the Essenes. Jesus did not so much teach this total dependence on God's grace as He proclaimed it in His conduct toward sinners. The principal significance, therefore, of what Jesus brings is not simply an advanced stage of the Essene view, but more accurately expressed, a different kind of view. More than this the discipline of comparative religions cannot determine.

Bultmann explains *the significance* of Jesus' statements by means of his *existential interpretation*. The radical demand and the corresponding total forgiveness express what Jesus means when He preaches: the kingdom of God is at hand. Such preaching is not really trying to announce a mythical world cataclysm, but seeks instead to loosen man from his manifold bondage to the world and history and thrust him into encounter with his neighbor. In this encounter with his neighbor man experiences what God wants of him and therein he acquires his genuine, as opposed to his previous inauthentic, history.[9] The foundation upon which Bultmann bases this interpretation is the outlook of existential philosophy that sees man as having forfeited his existence into bondage to the world and needing to be "saved" by regaining his own authentic existence.

But the foundation upon which Jesus Himself bases His view of man is God's covenant with Israel. Man is man

[8] H. Braun, *Spätjüdisch-häretischer und frühchristlicher Radikalismus* (Tübingen, 1957).

[9] Bultmann, *Theol.*, I, 25f.

under the Law. From this starting point Jesus then develops, in contrast to all the teachers of Israel, even Qumran's "teacher of righteousness," what God's commandment is, not by exegesis of the Law, but in *antithesis* to it. The antithetic form of Jesus' commandments in the Sermon on the Mount (Mt 5.20-48) accurately expresses His meaning even if, as appears likely, only three of the recorded six were expressed in precisely this form by Jesus Himself. Jesus places His admonitions in contrast to the commandments that God has given through Moses. He constitutes the newly promulgated demand of God in contrast with the old.

By means of this contrast *Jesus makes a distinction between the juridical law and the total commandment* both of which are somewhat merged in the Old Testament as well as in Judaism. We can make the observation that to some extent Jesus' new demands are already present in the Old Testament and in Judaism (e.g., thou shalt not covet), but then we notice that what He said "was said to the men of old" and frequently does not literally agree with any Old Testament commandment. For example, nowhere in the Old Testament do we find: "You shall love your neighbor and hate your enemy" (Mt 5.43). This statement is also unknown in rabbinic literature. Not until the DSS came to light (1 QS 1.9f.) was another instance of it finally found. However, Jesus' antithesis to this statement was not intended, as some scholars have hastily deduced, to express His opposition to the Essenes. What Jesus intends thereby is to circumscribe the intention of the commandments of Moses. In the Old Testament "the neighbor" mentioned in the commandment is one "of your own people" and "the stranger sojourning with you" (Lev 19.18,33f.). Thus Qumran represents a radicalizing of one possibility of the Old Testament commandment to love the neighbor, a radicalization in terms of the order of retribution whereby God loves the elect and the righteous and is wrathful with the sinners. For Jesus, however, the neighbor may be any man who needs to be shown love even if that man is an enemy of God and of God's people. For God Himself seeks the sinners even though He inexorably condemns sin. Thus the demands of God that Jesus proclaims are in accordance with His echatological redemptive work. From this position He has a clearer view of the genuine character of the Mosaic commandments than the Old Testament itself or even Judaism itself had. With His antitheses Jesus highlights two aspects of the Mosaic commandments: (1) they are judicially practicable regulations, and (2) they presuppose evil as a power which the Law can contain but cannot remove.

The dispute about divorce (Mk 10.2-9 par. Mt) makes this even more apparent. Moses had written the divorce commandment because of "your hardness of heart" (Mk 10.5). Therefore Jesus' injunction against divorce will not become an actual possibility until the "hardness of heart" is removed. As the prophets predicted, such a removal would not occur until the era of salvation (Ezek 36.26). Consequently Jesus' demands would be meaningless if He Himself did not produce that renewal of the heart promised for the time of salvation.

When seen in this light Jesus' new demand has a different relationship to the eschaton, to the kingdom of God, from that which has been consistently held since the investigations of Albert Schweitzer. The new demand is conditioned, not by the nearness, but by the presence, of the eschaton. The eschaton is present wherever the prophetic word is being fulfilled. In keeping with the terminology of both the Old Testament and Judaism, "kingdom of God" in Jesus' thought surely means a new world. But for Him the new world does not begin with a transformation of the cosmos or of political affairs. It begins with the transformation of the heart, that is, with the new relationship between God and man (Mt 11.2-6).

This change of heart takes place wherever Jesus grants His fellowship to men and therewith transposes them to discipleship, to faith, to repentance. When this happens the beatitude of the poor is being fulfilled: "theirs is the kingdom of heaven."

If we appropriate this *heilsgeschichtlich* perspective of Jesus for ourselves we can summarize the relationship between His and Judaism's views on God's demands and God's forgiveness as follows:

1. Jesus' demands are not only in antithesis to Jewish exegesis of the law,[10] but also to the Mosaic Law itself. The meaning of the antithesis is not to propose a better law or a higher morality alongside of the law of Israel, but to bring this law to fulfillment (Mt 5.17). That means that the will of God that stands behind this law is now to be realized as it was intended to be realized and now can be realized in the time of fulfillment, the time of salvation. By means of the antithesis Jesus, on the one hand, *exposes the character of the law* in a way that the Old Testament had not yet achieved,[11] namely, it is a limited regulation within the relative order of retribution. It presupposes evil as essentially invincible, but nevertheless at the same time calls attention to God's unconditional demand (Mk 12.28-31). On the other hand, Jesus thereby characterizes His own demand. His is not a worthy ideal that men ought to strive for, but it is the apodictic commandment of that God who

[10] Jesus does not follow the exegetical tradition of the scribes (Mt 7.29). For Martin Dibelius this is the decisive difference. See his book *Jesus*, p. 126.

[11] Jewish historians have emphasized for a long time that Paul misunderstood the Torah (cf. H. J. Schoeps, *Paul. The Theology of the Apostle in the Light of Jewish Religious History* [London, 1961], pp. 218, 261f.). In recent years Old Testament scholarship has seen even more clearly that the picture of the Torah which Paul constructs is hardly to be found in the Old Testament (cf. v. Rad, II, 402-24 [German]). In actual fact it is a new picture. Here too Paul is giving theological expression to something that had occurred by virtue of Jesus' ministry (cf. Chap. XI, note 11).

is now setting up his dominion and making his ultimate judgment upon evil.

2. *Jesus' demands are not law, but they are expressions of His call to repentance in concrete cases.* They call for repentance because the kingdom of God is coming. They are initially *judgmental words of repentance.* The form of some of the antithetic demands is actually taken from the condemnatory sentence structure of casuistic jurisprudence (Mt 5.22,28,32). They condemn "hardness of heart." But for everyone who encounters Jesus' work of salvation they become a saving call to repentance. Contrary to what Bultmann says, the content of Jesus' demands is not simply a call to demonstrate love of neighbor. Instead they call for discipleship and faith.[12] Faith here means that in confrontation with Jesus' work a man acknowledges the justice of God's judgment and seeks God's help in Jesus. Discipleship (following Jesus) and faith are the consummation of repentance and return to God. This return to God subsequently also manifests itself in impeccable marital fidelity or in demonstrations of love to every man whom God allows to confront us as our neighbor.

3. *The consequence of this is that the fulfillment of the demands of Jesus does not consist in man's making a decision for God, but in Jesus' own work of salvation.* When Jesus calls Levi the tax collector to follow Him, He is granting him His own fellowship and with that fellowship a new relationship to God. Levi then lives out his discipleship by acting in accordance with his new God-relationship day in and day out (Mk 2.14 par.). In another instance when Jesus grants His fellowship to the tax collector Zacchaeus, Zacchaeus repents (Lk 19.6ff.).

4. *Accordingly we see that Jesus not only sets His message in contrast to the Law, but He actually in His own*

[12] E. Schweizer, *Lordship and Discipleship* (London, 1960). It is significant that not until recent years was the new discovery made within the Bultmann school that discipleship and faith play a central role in Jesus' work. Bultmann himself had given both next to no consideration at all.

person becomes the Law's successor. The Law declared that participation in salvation was dependent on fulfilling the Law. Jesus made participation in salvation dependent on one's connection with His own person. Thus Jesus replaces the Law as the mediator between God and man. His yoke replaces the yoke of the Law (Mt 11.28ff.). It is because of this replacement of mediators and not merely logical necessity that *repentance and forgiveness are inseparable.* Because of the different mediator, forgiveness is not some kind of canceled note that one can display as evidence of a paid-up debt. Because the mediators have changed, no one has God's salvation unless he believes that it is *there* for him in Jesus. And therewith the words forgiveness and repentance which Jesus appropriated together with other Jewish theological terms are filled with completely new meaning.

5. *Finally, with reference to Jesus' own person the conclusion is inescapable: Jesus is not, as Bultmann thinks, similar to John the Baptist, one who merely conveys the final word of God.* But of Jesus it must be said that, if His demands as well as His fellowship with sinners and finally His entire work are to have any meaning at all, He is that one through whom man's relationship with God is ultimately and conclusively made whole. The Jesus who in this way effected complete fellowship with God while annulling the Law can be none other than that "bringer of salvation" who was to come in the last days. But in moving on now to consider the question of Jesus' messianic consciousness it is not of prime importance to determine whether and in what sense Jesus laid claim to any messianic titles. What is much more important is whether Jesus claimed to be doing God's last and final work of salvation, and in what sense He had authority to do it. Until this question is answered, the argument over messianic titles is altogether meaningless. And so we are left with the same question that disturbed the Jews: By what authority do you do these things?

Chapter V

The Offense to Judaism: The Hidden Nature of Jesus' Authority

1. The Mercifully Hidden Nature of the End-Time Revelation

There was nothing in the resources of Judaism that would have led anyone to acknowledge Jesus' authority. That Jesus' activity constituted *the fulfillment of law and promise* could not be proved, not even from scripture and especially not from Judaism's one-sided interpretation of it. Only that faith which had forsaken the resources of Judaism discovered it. For this reason Jesus gave no "scriptural proof" such as Justin Martyr tried. Jesus simply but continually announced that what scripture had promised as the culmination of salvation was now taking place, even though it was hidden and done by signs. Mt 11.4f. records: "Tell John what you hear and see: the blind receive their sight and the lame walk, . . . the dead are raised up, and the poor have good news preached to them." What this says is that those things which the Old Testament prophecy announced for the future time of salvation were now taking place. Yet viewed externally, little more was happening in Jesus' ministry than in the days of Elijah—a scattered few were provisionally being healed and called back into this world. No one could see that here the new world free of sorrow and death was dawning unless he had heard Jesus say: "Your faith has saved you" and had understood that here his relationship with God had been cured and made whole. Even Jesus' preaching when viewed externally appeared no different from the prophets' call to repentance and their promises of salvation. No one could see that this preaching was gospel, that is, the message whereby God sets up His salutary dominion (Is 52.7), unless he was one "who takes no offense at Jesus," but face to face with Jesus acknowledged the justice of God's verdict. Only such a person could understand all of Jesus' references to the typological fulfillment of redemptive history: "Behold, something greater than the temple is here," "greater than Jonah"—namely, "he who is to come"!

For all the rest, however, even Jesus' miracles, including the empty tomb and His Easter appearances, as well as His corresponding conquest of sin were no demonstrable proof that the new world was dawning. Unbelievers could still explain His miracles as demonic (Mk 3.22 par.; Mt 9.34). In responding to them (Mk 3.23-27; Mt 12.25-30 par. Lk) Jesus did not try to refute their explanation logically but simply tried to make them aware of the total decision involved in the situation. Jesus' "miracles," since they are part and parcel of the work of Him who seeks to save the lost by faith, can only be seen as the salutary signs that they are by those who are in that faith.

Therefore anyone who wanted to evaluate Jesus' authority from the presuppositions of Judaism had to demand from Him a sign from heaven, a miracle clearly from God (Mk 8.11-13 par. Mt; Mt 12.38ff. par. Lk). The demand for a sign was Judaism's distinctive demand on Jesus (1 Cor 1.22), no matter which branch of "this generation" (Mk 8.12 par.) was making it.[1] Marginal references most often name the Pharisees. Judaism, because of its very essence, had to demand this sign, for in the last analysis it was expecting from God and from His Messiah, whatever sort He might be, a demonstration of His power to carry out the Law. But by the same token, Jesus, because of the

[1] Cf. Jn 2.18; 6.30. Any prophet who does not follow the exegetical tradition must authenticate himself by miracles (*Billerbeck*, I, 726f.; II, 480).

very essence of His mission, could give no such sign from God to convince the unbelievers, for it was through the "weakness" of *sola gratia* (by grace alone), along with the abolition of the Law, that He came to save believers (1 Cor 1.21). Thus the only sign Jesus could announce was "the sign of Jonah" (Mt 12.39 par. Lk; Mt 16.4; cf. Jn 2.19), that someone would come to "this generation" who had gone through death itself. This did not refer to His post-Easter appearances, but to the Son of man's coming for judgment. When the Son of man comes in power to judge the world according to the Law and visibly to save the faithful (Lk 12.8f.), it will then be shown that He did have the "authority" to abrogate the Sabbath and "to forgive sins" (Mk 2.10, 28 par.).

Until that time, however, no "scriptural proof" and no "miracle" could uncover the hidden authority of Jesus (Mk 11.27-33 par.), but only submission to His call to repentance. Consequently the gracious concealment of Jesus' authority became a blinding veil to the Jews who were unrepentant (cf. Jn 5.31-47; 7.17).

2. *The Condemning Veil Before the Messiahship of Jesus*

Before any discussion about His messiahship could arise, Jesus veiled His actual office from the unrepentant. Jesus veiled "the secret of the kingdom of God," which is the presence of that kingdom in his person and his work—in other words, his messiahship—in "riddles" (Mk 4.10-12 par.). This passage is a saying of Jesus which is independent from the parable. Mk 4.10 par. reveals the connecting thread. Therefore it needs to be interpreted apart from its context with the parable and from the varying interpretations of the evangelists, and only in connection with the subject involved, namely, the "*messianic secret*." According to Mark's gospel Jesus disclosed His messiahship only to

His disciples and then forbade their spreading this secret publicly until His ministry was concluded (Mk 8.30 par.; 9.9 par. Mt). But even they misunderstood Him right down to the very end (Mk 4.40f. par.; 6.52; 8.17; 8.21 par. Mt; 9.10, 32 par. Lk; 14.37 par. Mt; 14.50 par. Mt). Even previous to this He had forbidden the circulation of reports about His miracles (Mk 1.44 par.; 5.43 par. Lk; 7.36; 8.26). The absence of parallel passages in Matthew and especially in Luke shows that this notion of Jesus' hiding His actual office from the public recedes in their presentations although there are still isolated instances of it in John (10.24). When historical critical scholarship discovered this notion uniquely in Mark's gospel and summarized it with the label "messianic secret,"[2] it appeared that this messianic secret was Mark's own private theory.[3] Apparently the evangelist was seeking to explain by this theory why Jesus' earthly career had no messianic character, whereas the historical reality in this case was that Jesus actually had not considered Himself to be the Messiah. More careful investigation, however, has now shown that Mark did indeed expand the messianic secret to a theory, but that *in nuce* the secret is also to be found completely independent of Mark in the Q tradition,[4] and that most important it characterizes precisely *the essential nature of Jesus' earthly career.* Up until the very end of His ministry Jesus never publicly made any claim to messiahship. The only messianic title that came from His lips, "Son of man," was one that He always used in the third person, as if He were speaking about someone else. In addition this term literally means no more than "man in general." Even when Jesus called attention to the scriptures being fulfilled, He did so in

[2] W. Wrede, *Das Messiasgeheimnis in den Evangelien* (Göttingen, 1901). For a summary of Wrede's thesis see V. Taylor (Chap. III, note 7), pp. 122ff.

[3] Thus Bultmann, *Theol.* I, 32, and G. Bornkamm, pp. 169ff.

[4] E. Sjöberg, *Der Verborgene Menschensohn in den Evangelien* (Lund, 1955).

indirect fashion. So He actually did speak in "riddles," and in Mk 4.12 the concept "parable" itself carries the connotation of the Hebrew word "*mashal*" (i.e., a proverb or figurative sentence).

What was *the purpose of this veiling?* It is reminiscent of an esoteric concern. The Essenes, for example, strictly forbade anyone revealing their distinctive teachings to outsiders. Jesus' disciples, however, had not been let in on secret esoteric wisdom, but had been recipients of the knowledge of faith. The disciples were believers, not "wise men," and therefore they themselves were plagued by doubt and misunderstanding again and again. The messianic secret is not something esoteric, *but it is a form of the hidden character of revelation for faith.* Precisely because of the nature of His messiahship Jesus was unable to make any open claim to messiahship. He was not looking for some external acknowledgment based, for example, upon His miracles, which would admit, "you must be the Messiah," but never got around to the repentance, faith, and discipleship which He sought to create. Therefore He could not confess that He really was the promised One to anyone else except those who were in His discipleship, not to the people at large. If He had openly admitted that He was the Messiah, this meaningless formal claim would have brought His career to a premature end. However, this veiling in the messianic secret must not be seen as a tactical move, for it is an elemental expression of the mercifully hidden nature of God's final revelation, which is at the same time, however, the blinding veil to all who do not believe.

How was this *negative side of the veiling* meant? The evangelists evaluate the tradition of the veiling differently, as is evident from the passage about riddles. They try to use it as an explanation of Israel's unbelief. According to Mark, Jesus Himself directly caused Israel's blindness by forbidding His disciples to instruct the people. For Mark the purpose of Jesus' veiled talk was to blind the Jews. For Matthew their blindness was the reason the words were veiled to them, though the blindness had been effected by God beforehand. Thereby Matthew sees more accurately than Mark that what was involved was not information about the things of God, but the unfolding of the final revelation for faith. Jesus granted this revelation to His church (Mt 13.16f.), but refused it to the mass of Israel because they closed their eyes in unbelief (Mt 13.13), actually because God had hardened their hearts (Mt 13.14f.). As a matter of fact, although Mark conceals this, during His days on earth Jesus' invitation to repent went openly to everyone, but the reason behind it was hidden.[5] This reason was revealed only to those who repented, and to the unrepentant it remained an offense. Whether the messianic secret is revealed to a person through repentance and faith, or whether he is condemned to have it hidden from him, in either case it is God's act and—though this is minimized in Matthew—Jesus' work, even though it all takes place in human decision (Mt 11.25-27 par. Lk; cf. 16.17; Jn 9.39-41).

3. *The Split*

Blinded to the real meaning of Jesus' claim, Judaism, if it wanted to remain Judaism, could only reject Jesus as one who blasphemously abolished the Law (Mk 2.7; 3.6 par.). In view of this fundamental break with Judaism as such, the indifference or wavering sympathy of broad segments of Jewish society was insignificant. Equally insignificant was the political apprehension of the governor of Galilee.[6]

Whoever *followed Jesus' call*, therefore, *forsook Judaism* not for reasons of historical expediency or on the spur of the moment, but in principle as a way of life before God. The new situation, however, always took the single form of

[5] "Those outside" in Mk 4.11 are like "the world" in Jn 1.10f.—in the first place all mankind.

[6] S. Perowne, The Later Herods (London, 1958).

82

fellowship with Jesus, whose mediatorial role replaced that of the Law. It was this fellowship factor which limited the actualization of Jesus' invitation during His days on earth to a small group. Jesus created the circle of the twelve (Mk 3.13-19 par.) as his witnesses to Israel and as a sign, an advance demonstration, of the new people of God (Mt 19.28; cf. Rev 21.12ff.). The actual people of God of the end-time could not come into existence until Jesus' exaltation, when through the Spirit He could grant His fellowship to all.

To the disciples Jesus' secret was revealed, since they were the few who perceived. It was in the name of the twelve that Peter, contrary to all apocalyptic ideas about the coming of the kingdom and disregarding all Jewish messianic concepts, *acknowledged Jesus to be the Messiah*, the culmination of redemptive history, the bringer of the final salvation (Mk 8.27-30 par.). Jesus accepted this confession and at the same time combined it with the announcement of suffering: "The Son of man must be rejected and suffer many things and after three days rise again."[7] Therewith the picture of a messiahship hidden from Israel was completed, though it would not be filled in until He reached Jerusalem. Jesus' whole knowledge of His mission, His attitude toward the Law and toward prophecy led to the announcement of suffering. On the other hand, the self-understanding of Judaism completely excluded the expectation of a suffering and dying Messiah such as Jesus.[8]

[7] This statement may well constitute the historical nucleus of the passion predictions. See Michaelis' article πάσχω, *TWNT*, V, 912-15.

[8] It was common knowledge in Jesus' Jewish environment that the righteous man must suffer and that God would exalt him. But no one ever thought of the promised One suffering and dying. Thus *Billerbeck*, II, 273-99 and Sjöberg (note 4), pp. 255-73. For a contrary opinion see J. Jeremias' article παῖς δεοῦ in *TWNT*, V, 680-98. Article also published as W. Zimmerli and J. Jeremias, *The Servant of God* ("Studies in Biblical Theology," No. 20; Naperville, Ill., 1957).

Chapter VI

The Decision in Jerusalem: Israel's Rejection of the Christ

1. The Historical Question of Who Crucified Jesus[1]

The New Testament writers unanimously name the Jews as the instigators of the crucifixion. According to the gospels, the leaders of the Jewish people delivered Jesus to the Roman procurator Pilate, and under pressure from them he sentenced Him against his own legal judgment. Before this, at least according to Mark and Matthew, Jesus was condemned by a trial before the Sanhedrin.

A self-righteous misuse of this New Testament presentation has been the basis for despising and persecuting the Jewish people through the centuries as the people who murdered Christ. For a hundred years Jewish research on Jesus has been trying to disprove this by means of historical criticism. Its contention is that the evangelists' reports concerning Jesus' condemnation by the Sanhedrin, as well as the pressure on Pilate, are not historical. Only the Roman and a clique of Jewish nobility in conspiracy with him were responsible for Jesus' crucifixion; it was not the Jewish people, least of all the Jewish religion.[2]

Protestant historical criticism has come to very similar conclusions. The classic work was H. Lietzmann's investigation of Jesus' trial.[3] We shall mention briefly his four arguments against the historicity of the report in Mark par. Matthew concerning the Jews' trial of Jesus: (a) Mk 14.55-

[1] A historically reliable account is J. Blinzler, The Trial of Jesus (Westminster, Md., 1959).

[2] Ibid, pp. 3-21.

[3] Sitzungsbericht der Berliner Akademie der Wissenschaften (Berlin, 1931), pp. 313-22.

65, he said, is a duplication of Mk 15.1, and the parallel passages are editings of Mark's report. In response to this it must be said that Mk 14.55-65 may well be a parallel transmission of Mk 15.1, but to all appearances the pericope does contain reliable information, since Jesus' condemnation by the Sanhedrin is also mentioned in the ancient summaries in Mk 8.31; 10.33; Lk 17.25; Acts 4.10; 13.27. The parallel passages in Luke and John, which report only an inquiry, can be better explained thus: The report of Luke concerning the trial is an editing of Mark's report; Luke's special sources probably had no information on it. John often anticipated parts of the passion story; he reported the Jewish leaders as condemning Jesus in direct connection with Jesus' active ministry. (b) The trial, Lietzmann said, contradicted the judicial procedures of the Mishnah. But this was an "unprecedented" trial, and the judicial procedures to which he refers were actually not set down until later. (c) He stated that the Sanhedrin, contrary to Jn 18.31 and the traditional interpretation, was indeed able to put a man to death; but crucifixion was a Roman punishment. Therefore Jesus could have been condemned only by the Romans. This thesis prompted a lengthy debate about the Sanhedrin's area of competence, which ultimately established the great probability of the traditional interpretation. Thus there remains only (d), Lietzmann's contention that the report of the indictment against Jesus arose from the circumstances of the later church. This can be answered only by viewing the context of the whole situation.

How one understands the cause of the crucifixion depends not on the historicity of individual reports about the proceedings against Jesus, but rather on one's total view of Jesus' relationship to Judaism. In its chief characteristics, the passion history of the gospels proves itself to be the logical conclusion of the controversy between Jesus and Judaism, as we have presented it so far.

85

2. *Jesus Forces the Decision*

During His entire public activity Jesus forced the Jews to a decision about Him; His final move in this direction was *His entry into Jerusalem*, which was not necessarily His only encounter with the city. The prophet from Galilee neither could nor would come to the Passover at Jerusalem as a private individual. For Him Jerusalem was the city of Judaism which killed the prophets but was nevertheless the city where redemption would dawn (Mt 23.37ff. par. Lk; Lk 13.33).

Jesus entered Jerusalem with the accompanying band of pilgrims in such a way that the cry welcoming the Messiah into David's city would echo around Him and that He would receive this homage as the "gentle and lowly" one, riding on an ass. For outsiders, this event was no proclamation of messiahship, but it did make the question of Jesus' messiahship more prominent than ever before.

More decisive than His entry was the *cleansing of the Temple* (Mk 11.15-19 par.; cf. Jn 2.13-17). This is not historically conceivable at any point except at the end of His career. Through this cleansing Jesus finally asserted His position toward the Law. Outwardly, it was simply prophetic intervention where a provision of the Law was being misused. But the loosely inserted word of explanation (Mk 11.17 par.) interprets the incident more pertinently in the light of Jesus' consistent attitude toward the Law. "You have made the temple a den of robbers." What was the Jew's misuse of the Law? With its help he concealed his wickedness. The Temple should be "a house of prayer (for all the nations)"; the offer of the grace of God should put man to work for God. It was already inherent in the insight of the prophets and certainly in Jesus' attitude toward the Law, that His prophetic demand would not be fulfilled by the Temple made with hands, any more than by the Law written on stone tablets. Jesus' repetition of the action and the demand of the prophets makes sense only if this prophetic cleansing of the Temple was a sign of the messianic renewal of the Temple, and if behind it all actually stood that of which the Sanhedrin accused Jesus (Mk 14.58; cf. Jn 2.18f.).

The appearance of the prophet Jesus in Jerusalem, surrounded as it was by the whole Messiah question, forced the Jewish leaders to declare themselves. If they would not follow the call to repentance directed toward them in the argument about authority (Mk 11.27-33 par.) and in the parable of the vineyard (Mk 12.1-12 par.), and would not give up their Judaism, they would have to expel Jesus from Judaism.

3. *The Son of Man Is "Delivered"*

The central *theme of the passion history* in the gospels is the word *"delivered"*: The Son of man was delivered by Judas to the Sanhedrin (Mk 14.10f. par.), by the Sanhedrin to Pilate (Mk 15.1, 10 par.), by Pilate to the soldiers to be crucified (Mk 15.15 par.). This does not diminish the decisive role of Pharisaism in rejecting Jesus, but rather views it in solidarity with everything encompassed by the word mankind.

The Crucifixion was carried out by the unknown mercenaries of those in power on this earth. But even the man in power, *Pilate*, seems to have been a prisoner of other powers. He tried to be judicially correct and yet act in accord with political necessities. This picture of Pilate as presented by the gospels is quite understandable, especially if the trial of Jesus, as is probable, took place after the overthrow of Pilate's powerful patron, Sejanus, in October of A.D. 31 Pilate sacrificed Jesus to preserve his own political position.

But "he who delivered me to you has the greater sin"

87

(Jn 19.11), namely, the Jew. Jesus was actually delivered by the *high priest* and his subordinates. The high priest saw in every messianic movement a threat to his own existence, and rightly so, as the outcome of the Jewish war shows. He too sacrificed Jesus to preserve his own social and political position, but thereby he disowned the mystery entrusted to his people. Therefore the guilt of the spiritual leaders of Israel was greater than that of the representative of worldly power.

The action of the Sadducees here certainly did not take place without consent of the Pharisees, as their first intervention against the early church did (see p. 104). Long before any political measures were taken, the Pharisees had made their basic decision against Jesus (see p. 69). The whole course of Jesus' controversy with them would lead one to expect just as unanimous a condemnation by the Sanhedrin as Stephen later met with.

(The *similarity between the two trials* can be explained not only from the history of traditions but also from actual history. Both times the condemnation was based on a statement about the Temple and a statement about the Son of man. The genuineness of Stephen's statements is unquestionable. In his words faith's own knowledge and tradition passed on from Jesus combine to create a confessional testimony. The very fact of such a confessional repetition of Jesus' self-testimony explains the monstrous effect Stephen's statements had on the Sanhedrin.)

The report of Jesus' *trial before the Sanhedrin* is, in any case, completely consonant with what was at issue. The accusation struck right at the heart of Jesus' whole activity. This was expressed in His statement about the Temple, a statement which was no longer quite clear to the church's tradition as passed on in the gospels, but for that very reason genuine,[4] and in His claim to messiahship which stood be-

[4] The statement is transmitted four times in the New Testament: Mk 14.58; Mt 26.61; Acts 6.14; Jn 2.19; cf. Mk 13.2. In each place it is formulated and interpreted differently.

hind everything. In making His Temple statement, Jesus was announcing that the Jews themselves, by their action against Him, would destroy the Temple, that sign of God's redemptive self-offering through law and promise, while Jesus would establish a new Temple, the perfected redemptive presence of God. The question about Jesus' *messiahship*, which seems to be tacked on rather disconnectedly, was internally closely connected with the first accusation. Renewal of the Temple is the work of the Messiah.[5] Jesus admitted that He was the Messiah, not in the sense that the high priest thought, but analogous to His whole activity: He was the Son of man, called to rule and judge the world with God's own authority. Therefore He had the authority to abolish both the Temple and the Law. This claim was blasphemy to the Jews, that an obviously powerless man who undermined the Law should claim God's dominion and judicial prerogatives for Himself.

Before Pharisaism delivered Him up, however, *Judas* did. He was "one of the twelve," and how much all of them shared his guilt was shown by their question when Jesus announced the betrayal: "Is it I?" (Mk 14.19 par. Mt; cf. Lk 22.23). The stumbling block for the disciples was Jesus' complete refusal to assert Himself by demonstrations of power, and His complete love which helped only others and not Himself and therefore led to suffering, as it inevitably had to. The man who would not serve and suffer but would rather assert himself, even if he stood at Jesus' right hand, betrayed the Son of man; but only those who strove for this self-assertion by means of God's law pressed for His execution (Jn 19.7).

The evangelists' contradictory statements about the *attitude of the people* clarify the sort of schizophrenia that brought forth this inevitable "no" of human nature toward Jesus. According to Matthew, the whole people expressly

[5] *Billerbeck*, I, 1005; IV, 929f.; O. Michel's article *ναός* in *TWNT*, IV, 888, 12ff.

agreed with the judgment of their leaders.[6] According to Luke's special tradition, the women of Jerusalem lamented the terrible fate of Jesus, without calling the judgment of their leaders unjust (Lk 23.27-32). The witnesses of Jesus' Crucifixion returned to the city shaken with remorse and fear (Lk 23.48). Joseph of Arimathea "had not consented to their purpose and deed" (Lk 23.51). In the same way devout Jews made great lamentation over Stephen, without being able to follow his belief (Acts 8.2). The same basic circumstances that appear in Luke as the tragedy of pious Israel appear in Matthew at the death of Judas (Mt 27.3-10): The man is overcome with remorse, pain, and fear at his deed, and yet cannot act otherwise (cf. Rom 7.13-25). *John's* gospel illuminates the real situation: "The Jews," as representatives of "the world," were compelled to bring about Jesus' death, even though Judaism itself was never without some doubt as to the justice of the act (Jn 7.45-52; 9.16; 11.49f.).

Jesus' encounter with Judaism thus proves to be a thoroughly historical event with far-reaching significance running beneath the surface. This becomes altogether apparent in considering its subsequent consequences for redemptive history.

[6] Mt 27.22 in contrast with par. Mk has the added word "all." So also Mt 27.25.

Chapter VII

Jesus' Own Pronouncement About Israel's Place in Redemptive History Following Its Rejection of Him

Jesus' own view of the conclusion of his earthly ministry should be briefly explained here. At the end of His career He did not simply expect the visible dawn of judgment and salvation as did the prophets until John the Baptist. He proclaimed not only the coming of the kingdom of God with its concommitant judgment upon all evil (Mt 4.17), but also the coming of the Son of man as judge of the world (Lk 12.8) as well as the rejection and the exaltation of the Son of man (Mk 8.31; 9.12; Lk 17.25). At first glance it is surprising that these *three pronouncements* are never tied together to each other but always appear separately. This observation has prompted Bultmann's school to conclude that only the proclamation of the kingdom is genuine with Jesus and that the assertions about the Son of man represent constructions of the early church. This is, they think, especially true of the passion predictions, all of which then are *vaticinia ex eventu*. On the contrary, the observation that the three strands remain separate can be explained only if all of them genuinely do arise from the situation of Jesus' earthly ministry. Jesus could not unite the future coming of the Son of man as judge of the world with the coming of the kingdom of God because both of them do not coincide. It is now in the present that "the kingdom of God has come upon you" (Mt 12.28)! By the same token He could hardly say that the Son of man must be rejected, rise again, and come as judge of the world. Such a combination would have contradicted the sense of both

91

pronouncements. Each is addressed to a different audience. The pronouncement that the Son of man as judge of the world will acknowledge those as His own who here have acknowledged Jesus in a public call to repentance. It makes clear to all that their response to Jesus determines their eternal destiny. The passion predictions, on the other hand, are always addressed to the disciples. Only to them do they make any sense. If we look at the original components of these predictions (p. 83) we see that they interpret Jesus' journey to Jerusalem for the disciples and promise them the concealed resurrection of Jesus. The resurrected Lord did indeed appear only to them. The passion predictions are surely much more than predictions about Jesus' own fate. They "teach" what "must" happen to the promised One according to God's redemptive plan proclaimed in the scriptures (cf. Lk 24.25ff.). They thus announce the conclusion of Jesus' ministry, and it is only from this conclusion that the entire ministry can be made meaningful.

If the nucleus of both of the pronouncements about the future of the Son of man actually originate with Jesus Himself, then Jesus also envisioned an *interim period between the death and resurrection* of the Son of man and His coming to judge the world. That is to say, Jesus envisioned *"the era of the church."*[1] When He instituted the Lord's Supper as His final passion prediction, He announced that earthly fellowship with Himself had come to an end and would be replaced with His offer of Himself as the one who died for all.[2] Jesus' understanding of the scriptures in correspondence with His understanding of Himself made this sort of idea imperative for Him, especially the idea that

---

[1] Some exegetes are of the opinion that Jesus expected the parousia to coincide with His resurrection. Evidence to the contrary showing that Jesus expected an interim period is to be found in W. G. Kümmel, *Promise and Fulfillment*, "Studies in Biblical Theology," No. 23; (Naperville, Ill., 1957), pp. 64ff.

[2] L. Goppelt's article πίνω in *TWNT*, VI, 141f.

God's final work of salvation was to save the many. Jesus bound salvation to His own person and concentrated in His earthly ministry on encountering Israel's leaders and on creating a close circle of disciples. This earthly ministry would have been completely meaningless if its conclusion were not also concentrated on Jesus' person, and if a time were not provided for the many to be saved, when the fellowship of the redeemed, portrayed in advance as a sign by the disciples, would be realized. This time of the church was to come after Jesus' departure and before the Son of man's visible revelation of power before the world!

It is against this general background that we must view and interpret Jesus' specific recorded statements about Israel's future following its rejection of Him.

1. *The Vineyard Is Taken Away*

In the Jews' rejection of Him Jesus saw not only the logical end to His controversy with them, but at the same time the consistent *conclusion of the conflict between God and Israel* that had existed ever since the establishment of their covenant relationship. Jesus Himself was this conclusion. He was the last in a long line of messengers sent by God. His coming marks the end of God's patient waiting. But even more than this, everything He did made Him the "finisher and perfecter," the One who fulfilled what had existed up until then by replacing it with something new. Consequently, after His rejection the Lord of the vineyard would "come and destroy the tenants, and give the vineyard to others" (Mk 12.9 par.). This sentence did not, like Mt 11.20-24; 12.41f., and Lk 13.6ff., proclaim universal judgment on persistent impenitence, but announced instead that what the prophets had threatened was now taking place in redemptive history, namely, the covenant people as such were being rejected (Mt 3.7-10). Giving the vineyard to others meant that after Jesus was rejected God would take another people and make them His covenant people. It is not absolutely certain whether this sentence still belongs to the original components of the vineyard parable. But properly understood it announces the same thing that other statements of Jesus envision, even if these latter are more restrained (Mt 8.12 par. Lk; Mk 11: 12ff. par. Mt).

One could understand the sentence in the manner of the Essene statements about Israel's covenant. Yet Jesus did not want to assert that now *God's covenant with Israel* would pass over to His followers, as the founder of the Qumran community claimed, so that Israel thereby became just another nation among the heathen nations with no special place in redemptive history. On the contrary, Jesus always viewed Israel as standing under Law and promise and placed His own followers under something new, which did not annul God's ordinance over Israel but did relegate it to being the "Old Covenant" (Mk 14.24; 1 Cor 11.25). Jesus founded a new relationship to God that replaced Israel's covenant relationship in the same way as Jesus' demand replaced the previously valid commandment and Jesus' forgiveness replaced the previously valid redemptive order. This was not just a succession in historical development, but succession in redemptive history. It is as though the new relationship dawning on a superior plane leaves Israel's covenant and Law far beneath it, even though they retain a validity until the end of this world. Israel remained the people of the covenant, but the covenant was no longer that one to be fulfilled by the coming Christ, but rather the one which was annulled by Him who did come, and therefore could be maintained only in opposition to Him or surrendered in favor of Him. Since something new was begun when Christ was rejected for the sake of the covenant (Mk 12.7), Israel's covenant faded away in redemptive history. Israel's worship, which was founded upon this fad-

94

ing covenant and which continued persistently in this attitude of refusing Jesus, was left hollow: "Behold, your house is forsaken and desolate" (Mt 23.38 par. Lk). "Your house," the Temple or the common life of Israel, would be forsaken by God. It would no longer be His house. The destruction of the Temple which Jesus envisioned in connection with this was simply an expression of this *removal of God's gracious presence.*[3] This judgment as the reverse side of the coin of the hidden final salutary revelation was not one that could be objectively verified. It could only be proclaimed: Any Jew who continues to seek salvation via Law and promise without reversing Israel's decision toward Jesus is grasping at straws. The sole source for saving fellowship with God is the Christ rejected by Israel. Salvation is offered by Christ's offering Himself in fellowship to those who have abandoned the way of salvation through the Law (Mk 14.22-24 par.). This is the unambiguous position expressed in Jesus' words, even though He naturally did not envision a history of the Jewish people which would continue for centuries characterized by these circumstances.

2. *The Salvation Still Awaiting Israel*

Rejecting the Christ encountered in one's own history, even crucifying Him, was not according to Jesus' own words the unforgivable sin of the disciple against the Holy Spirit. Even sins of such proportions are still sins against the Son of man and they can be forgiven (Mt 12.32). For this sort of sin Jesus' words apply: "Forgive them; for they know not what they do" (Lk 23.34). Consequently after Easter the apostles could once more call Israel to repentance in view of the salvation now completed in the Cross and Resur-

---

[3] Cf. p. 89. It is not accidental that this sign of the destruction of the Temple did not occur until the year 70 when Israel had herself invalidated the Temple by a rejection of the gospel which for the time being had all the marks of finality.

rection, especially since they themselves had all received forgiveness on Easter for their share of guilt in Jesus' cross.

Would Israel change its attitude after Jesus' death? Was there any other possibility for "this generation" which had rejected Jesus than that they would be worse off at the coming of the Son of man than the most godless heathen (Mt 11.20-23; 12.41ff.; 23.35f. par. Lk)? The final words of Jesus' condemnatory speech to Jerusalem look forward to the hour of a *redemptive encounter between Christ and Israel*: "You will not see me again, until you say, 'Blessed be he who comes in the name of the Lord' " (Mt 23.39 par. Lk). This does not refer to a terrified Israel paying homage to the One who appears for judgment (Mt 24.30, Rev 1.7), but rather to a converted Israel greeting Him with joy. Conversion is the condition for this redemptive encounter. The conversion Jesus has in mind here is a promising invitation, but not yet the promise of Rom 11.25f., which pertains even after the Jews have rejected the apostolic proclamation. However, this conversion stipulation does not mean that the redemptive encounter between Israel and its Christ is purely hypothetical. No, this encounter for salvation remains the final goal of God's ways. Jerusalem will eventually see its Christ, and it will be a blessed vision. We could not understand the intensity of the apostles' preaching to Israel after His departure unless we had recognized that Jesus Himself had given both the direction and promise for it. Its preliminary failure does not annul the promise of Jesus.

Part II.

The Church Breaks Away
from the Community of Israel:
Paul and Judaism

Preliminary Note on the Sources

1. The Acts of the Apostles is essentially neither a historical report nor a biased reconstruction of history.[1] It does not try to depict the beginnings of a historical phenomenon any more than the gospels do. It is much rather intent upon witnessing to the beginnings of the church, which only faith can see. Thus it presents tradition in kerygmatic fashion. Just as we do not look for the historical Jesus in the gospels, so here we do not look for the historical phenomenon that a disinterested bystander might have seen, but rather for the significance of the historical circumstances that was revealed only to faith. When we speak of the "significance" of the historical phenomena, we do not mean simply interpreting the meaning, as is possible and necessary with every historical event, but rather seeing the trans-historical event occurring "in, with, and under" the historical event. For example, Pentecost as a historical phenomenon is an outburst of enthusiastic behavior within a certain messianic Jewish sect. For faith, however, it is an event in redemptive history, the Spirit of the last days (Acts 2.17) moving into action and thereby laying the basic foundation for the new people of God. In this interpretive endeavor we must take

[1] Literature: (1) For presentations of the history of the apostolic age see H. Lietzmann, History of the Early Church, Vol. I, The Beginnings of the Christian Church (4th ed.; New York, 1961). C. T. Craig, The Beginning of Christianity (New York, 1943). G. B. Caird, The Apostolic Age (London, 1955). P. Carrington, The Early Christian Church, 2 vols. (Cambridge, 1957). L. Goppelt, Die Apostolische und Nachapostolische Zeit, Vol. I,A of Die Kirche in ihrer Geschichte (Göttingen, 1962), (2) For commentaries on Acts see F. J. Foakes-Jackson and K. Lake (eds.), The Beginnings of Christianity, Part I: The Acts of the Apostles. Vols. I-V (London, 1920ff.). C. S. Williams, A Commentary on the Acts of the Apostles (London, 1957). German commentaries include E. Haenchen's in the Meyer-Kommentar (12th ed.; Göttingen, 1959), G. Stählin's in Das Neue Testament Deutsch (Göttingen, 1962), and H. Conzelmann's in Handbuch zum Neuen Testament (Tübingen, 1963).

care to distinguish between the original event as faith saw it and the meaning it acquired in later presentation. This sort of critical approach to Acts can be undertaken only in pericopic fashion and not on the basis of source theories.

2. Besides general historical criteria, the historical data of the *Pauline letters* are especially helpful in this endeavor.

3. In addition, inferences that can be drawn from the *Book of Revelation* and from the *synoptic tradition*, especially according to Matthew, give information on the history of the Palestinian church.

Chapter VIII

The Church Moves Out to the Edges of Judaism

1. The Initial Position of the Early Church Toward Judaism

While His disciples panicked, deserting Him, and fleeing into hiding, Jesus died alone as a condemned man. A short time later in Jerusalem and probably also in Galilee a *fellowship of these disciples of Jesus* arose, gathered around this confession: "God has raised up the crucified One and exalted Him to His right hand. Because of Him God sends the Spirit of the end-time into action. The crucified One is God's promised One and as such He will appear in glory very shortly."[2] Notwithstanding this confession the fellowship remained as a matter of course *within the community of Israel* by strictly observing the Law, especially the rite of circumcision (Acts 3.1; 10.14; 21.20; Gal 2.3). To the outsider, early Christianity appeared to be one of the numerous Jewish movements or sects (Acts 24.5; 14; 28.22).

Historical criticism confused this *appearance* with the *essence of the group*, and throughout the nineteenth century propounded this view: "The earliest Christians were nothing else and wanted to be nothing else than a small gathering of messianic Jews," who sought to win fellow Jews over to their special confession by the quietest sort of propaganda. But in what sense then did they confess Jesus as the Messiah? With this question the *Religionsgeschicht-*

[2] The components of the four Petrine sermons in Acts 2-5 concur with the tradition in 1 Cor. 15.3-5. They present the oldest kerygma. Cf. C. H. Dodd, *The Apostolic Preaching and Its Developments* (7th ed.; London, 1951).

liche Schule (school of interpretations associated with the history of religions) moved beyond this modernizing conception of historical criticism. These scholars sought to explain primitive Christianity's self-awareness from the fact that is applied apocalyptic expectations to Jesus and His followers. When this was clarified theologically after 1918, it led to the insight, which has become practically common knowledge among scholars, that even the first Christians *knew themselves to be the church* in the deepest meaning of the term.[3] But even today the source of this consciousness remains largely unclarified.

The source of the primitive church's confessing Jesus as the Christ and thus the source of its self-awareness was not the dawning within the disciples of a belief in a resurrection which overcame the cross. Nor was it their explanation of the cross through messianic theories. The real source was *the resurrected One's self revelation and the apostles'* own eyewitness *Easter testimony.* The crucified One returned to them very much alive and with forgiving fellowship for the very disciples who had denied and deserted Him. The resurrected One renewed the apostolate. This testified that the crucified historical Jesus was the resurrected Christ.[4] Jesus' own proclamation moved toward the creation of the new covenant through the finale of His encounter with Israel, the cross and resurrection. The apostolic proclamation took its start from that point. The first was a hidden witness, the latter open testimony to Him as the bringer of salvation.[5]

[3] O. Linton, *Das Problem der Urkirche in der neueren Forschung* (Uppsala, 1932). G. Johnston, *The Church in the New Testament* (Cambridge, 1934). N. A. Dahl, *Das Volk Gottes, eine Untersuchung zum Kirchenbewusstsein des Urchristentums* (1941; reprinted Darmstadt, 1962).

[4] L. Goppelt, H. Thielicke, and H. R. Müller-Schwefe, *The Easter Message Today* (New York, 1964).

[5] A. von Harnack and many after him see a sharp break between Jesus' gospel which He Himself preached and the gospel of Jesus Christ

101

Separating early Christianity and Judaism was the two-fold confession that in the last analysis all were guilty of the Crucifixion, and that in cross and resurrection salvation had dawned. The kerygma of the church, arising from the apostolic witness to Easter, called the Jewish people to this confession. They were called to confess the redemptive meaning of cross and resurrection as illuminated by the scriptures, not to acknowledge some particular theories about Jesus. Founded on this kerygma the church did not regard itself, like the Pharisees or the Qumran sect, as the remnant of Israel destined for God's salvation.[6] Nor by any means did it regard itself as a new religion alongside the Jewish religion. Instead, in spite of all appearances, it regarded itself as the redeemed community of the end-time, distinct from Israel (Mt 16.18). It called the people of the old covenant over into the new covenant, across the boundary placed between old and new by the cross and resurrection of Jesus, although at this early stage it most likely did not make use of these concepts in doing so.

But did not the early Christians' position in practice lag far behind this initial impetus? How can we reconcile their continued observance of the law and the limitation of their proclamation to Israel with their new self-awareness and its source in the earthly career of Jesus now completed in His cross and resurrection? Initially the church was able to call Israel to repentance and into the new covenant merely by referring to Jesus' cross and resurrection. In these

---

which His disciples preached about Him. Harnack declared: Only the Father, not the Son belongs in the gospel as Jesus preached it! If, however, Jesus' forgiveness is, as we have clearly seen, bound to His person, then even the salvation which the earthly Jesus preached is already testimony to Himself. Then John is making a proper interpretation when in his gospel he replaces Jesus' offer of forgiveness with His offer of Himself as the truth and the life. Then the difference between Jesus' preaching and that of the apostles is finally determined in reference to the messianic secret. In the apostles' preaching the secret is unveiled (cf. Chap. V).

[6] J. Jeremias, "Der Gedanke des 'heiligen Restes,' etc.," ZNW, XLII (1949), 184ff.

initial stages it was not necessary to repeat Jesus' call to repentance in terms of the statutes of the Law nor, like Him, to break these statutes as a sign and witness to the new covenant. In their own position toward the Law they acted according to Mt 23.23b and 17.24-27, and were only careful to make sure that their righteousness exceeded that of the Pharisees (cf. Mt 5.20). Illustrative of this was their fellowship of love, absolutely unique in the history of religions and the history of the church (Acts 4.34-37). They had been set free for this new righteousness by placing their hope of salvation not on their own righteousness but solely on the promise that the Son of man, soon to appear in glory, would graciously acknowledge those who had humbly taken refuge in Him (Lk 12.8; Mt 25-37-40). Consequently it was precisely by virtue of their practical relationship toward the Law that they were profoundly separated from Judaism, even though it may not have been overtly perceptible, and though perhaps even they themselves were not conscious of it.

The same thing applies to *their position toward their universal mission*. The universal character of God's redemption had been announced in prophecy (Is 2.2ff.; 49.6) and unmistakably ordered when Jesus indicated that the salvation appearing in Him was meant for all peoples (Mt 8.11; 22.1-10; Mk 14.24).[7] Here, too, the primitive church did not set up programs of action, but obediently acted as God's timetable dictated. On the basis of Old Testament promise their initial expectation could only be that salvation would come to all peoples through a converted Israel. So they felt constrained to concentrate their proclamation on Israel. That God's way was different, as the cross had intimated in advance, was unknown to the Christians until they saw Israel's reaction to their message.

[7] J. Jeremias, *Jesus' Promise to the Nations* (London, 1957).

2. The Position of Judaism Toward the Jerusalem Congregation

According to the report in Acts many were won for the message, even from the upper classes (Acts 2.47; 6.7; 9.31; 21.20). But before very long not only the indifferent and fickle masses, but also the nucleus of those consciously representing Judaism proved to be more and more inaccessible. How did that Judaism which remained *Judaism act toward the church?* Luke does not report what befell Christians here and there in the synagogues of the land. This may be reflected in Mt 10.17-23. Luke characterizes only the ultimately crucial situation in Jerusalem (Acts 4.1-31; 5.17-42). At first the Jerusalem congregation remained unmolested. Not until a specific occasion prompted Peter and John to proclaim their message publicly in the Temple were they arrested by the captain of the Temple, "because they were proclaiming in Jesus the resurrection from the dead" (Acts 4.1-3). The intervention was thus initiated by the Sadducean priestly nobility whose most prominent representative was, next to the high priest, the captain of the Temple. Proclaiming the resurrection of someone condemned by the Sanhedrin struck the priestly nobility as an act of religious fanaticism endangering the existing order and undermining their authority (Acts 5.28). The apostles were arraigned before the Sanhedrin. Since they were "uneducated men" (not formally trained in the Law) (Acts 4.13) and since the miracle had won the heart of the people, the Sanhedrin released them with a warning forbidding any further preaching of this sort.[8] The disciples did not obey this injunction and when subsequently brought

[8] The action follows Jewish law. In such cases those unaware of the law first had to be warned before they could be punished. (See J. Jeremias, "Untersuchungen zum Quellenproblem der Apostelgeschichte," *ZNW*, XXXVI (1937), 205-21, 209ff.) It must also be kept in mind that chapters 4 and 5 of Acts belong to two different strata of tradition.

before the Sanhedrin again they once more indicated that they would persist in this attitude (Acts 5.17f.; 28-32). Consequently the Sadducean priestly nobility was determined to do away with them (Acts 5.33). But Gamaliel asserted the Pharisees' viewpoint. He demanded the same course of action in regard to the disciples of Jesus as had proved good in the case of messianic movements among the Zealots. Thus only a scourging was inflicted upon the apostles as punishment, most likely for their disobedience (Acts 5.40; cf. Mt 10.17). Actually it was not because of their fanatic religious views, but chiefly because of their professing them in public, that the disciples were indicted. Thus we can understand why the apostles and especially also the other members of the church remained essentially unmolested after that.

This picture of the circumstances is surprising. *Historical criticism* declared it to be completely unhistorical. Could the Pharisees, the bitter enemies of Jesus, intercede for the toleration of His followers? Was not the only reason for the church's being relatively unchallenged during the early days that it kept in the background? In point of fact, however, the representatives of Judaism also must have encountered the existence and claims of the Jerusalem congregation. They responded by rejecting it with unnerving nonchalance, and otherwise actually did act essentially the way Luke described it. This is confirmed by Josephus' report—in this case, hardly suspect—concerning the killing of James, the Lord's brother (*Ant.*, 20,9,1). This action too was initiated by a Sadducean high priest, and the Pharisees and the people condemned it because it struck out against the man who had been well known for his pious observance of the Law. In this messianic movement, as in every other, the Sadducean priestly nobles saw a threat to their political position. The Pharisees, however, because of their own fear of God, refused to acknowledge political expediency as grounds for doing away with pious and law-abiding heretics.

3. The Church Breaks Through the Boundaries of Judaism

This position of the Pharisees was destined to undergo a fundamental change when *Stephen* was brought before the Sanhedrin accused of having said: "Jesus of Nazareth will" (at his future coming) "destroy this place" (the Temple), "and will change the customs which Moses delivered to us" (that is, the whole observance of ceremonial legality connected with the Temple) (Acts 6.14). This accusation was "false" (Acts 6.13) only because of the accusers' tendentious insinuation of blasphemy. The *defense* which Stephen makes in his justification intends to show that his actual assertion did not tend toward blasphemy. He denounces Israel's history: *God's redemptive presence was not limited to the Temple* (Acts 7.44-50), but had been granted to the fathers in the most varied places (7.33). Circumcision, the foremost of the customs of Moses (Acts 21.21), had not diminished the constant opposition which the circumcised showed toward God and His messengers, but only hidden it (7.8,51). Through the infamy of Jacob's sons (Acts 7.9ff.; cf. 4.27f.), God inaugurated the time of promise in spite of Israel's opposition (7.17). Whereas Peter called the sons of the prophets to God's salvation (Acts 3.25ff.), Stephen called the sons of the prophets' murderers (7.52) to the salvation that was nevertheless prepared for them. Jesus' relationship to the Old Testament, therefore, was not only grounds for inviting Judaism, but also for separating from it. Evidently before the conflict came to a head Jews had rejected Stephen's preaching with express references to Israel's place in redemptive history. Therefore he declared that *neither the Temple nor membership in the cultic community would save them from*

106

the wrath due to break upon them when Jesus appeared. It was not liberal tendencies of Hellenistic Judaism[9] which stood *behind his declaration*, but rather *Jesus' own preaching of repentance*. Nor was it the spirit of Hellenistic enlightenment, but the Spirit of Jesus which took the lead in breaking through the boundaries of Judaism, while Judaism retreated within itself. Judaism rejected Stephen's preaching as an attack on the foundations of its existence. Because of his speech before the Sanhedrin, Stephen, without being formally sentenced but in accordance with the will of all (Acts 7.57), was tumultuously cast out of the community as a blasphemer and stoned (7.58).

4. *The Persecution Which Arose over Stephen and Its Effects*

The stoning of Stephen was followed by a *persecution* of the Jerusalem congregation (Acts 8.1-3). If the church's teaching led to such conclusions, which touched the very foundations of Judaism, then it too had to be eliminated from the Jewish community just as Jesus was. Zealous for the Law, according to his own statement (Gal 1.13f.), Paul as a Pharisee took part in this.

According to Acts 8.1, all the members of the church except the apostles were supposed to have fled. It is improbable that the leaders of the church, who were, of course, especially in danger, should remain behind alone. Actually Acts continues to presuppose a congregation in Jerusalem,

[9] Stephen is the most outstanding representative of the Hellenists (Acts 6.1). In Jerusalem those congregational members were labeled Hellenists whose native tongue was Greek. They came from the circle of Diaspora Jews who had settled in Jerusalem and formed their own synagogue congregations (Acts 6.9). Because of their presence, the gospel had already been translated into the Greek language in Jerusalem. Besides that they were of considerable importance in developing the mission and theology of primitive Christianity. But they were not a separate theological party founded on the spirit of Hellenistic enlightenment as has been asserted time and time again in historical research. See M. Simon, *St. Stephen and the Hellenists* (London and New York, 1958).

107

without indicating any new beginning. On the other hand, the ones who fled and are later mentioned by name were all Hellenists (Acts 8.4; 11.19). Therefore it was probably only the Hellenists close to Stephen who really forsook Jerusalem for good, while not only the apostles but also all the rest of the members of the congregation after a short period of seclusion continued to live in Jerusalem as before. Of course the persecution was not directed only toward the Hellenists. Paul never indicates that he persecuted only one group of Christians. The unorganized purge was naturally first directed against those known to be friends of Stephen. Above all, however, those who shared the insights of Stephen had more reason to avoid a subpoena before Jewish courts than those who held fast to the Law in every respect. The latter could probably move about unhindered again in Jerusalem soon after the first storm was over (Acts 9.31).

Thus it was at this time, but not before this, that two wings of primitive Christianity arose, divided on the point Stephen had raised, namely, the central position of Jesus' preaching of repentance. One wing, the believers remaining in Jerusalem, thought they had to relegate this side of Jesus' proclamation to the background because of their own conscience scruples, and in order to continue living and working within the Jewish community. For them keeping the Law, which initially had been congregational practice unconsciously pursued as a matter of course, now became increasingly a conscious matter of principle (cf. Acts 21.20). For this reason they remained essentially unmolested, especially since the Roman procurators following Pontius Pilate after the year 36 no longer allowed the Jews any self-jurisdiction. It is in character with the above-mentioned situation that even Pharisaic circles should welcome it when Agrippa I, to whose kingdom Jerusalem belonged between 41 and 44, set out to execute the anticipated judgment of God upon these heretical fanatics (Acts 12). After his sudden death the

108

Jerusalem congregation continued to live in the Jewish community under the peaceful order maintained by the Romans up until the beginning of the Jewish war. Thus remaining within the Jewish folk-community they were mistrusted by the Sadducees, tolerated by the Pharisees, and respected by the people (Acts 21.17-20).

The other wing consisted of the believers who, with Stephen, also upheld the negative side of Jesus' call to repentance in order to give the gospel its full sharpness. These were forced not only beyond the geographical boundaries of Palestinian Jewish communities, but also *beyond the boundaries of Judaism* itself. Thus by the course of the events they were shown the initially hidden way which God had in mind for calling the nations of the world.

Chapter IX

The Church Inside and Outside Judaism

1. *The Problem of Gentile Missions*

From the very beginning the primitive church was certain that the salvation which had appeared in Jesus was meant for the whole world, but the *how* was hidden from them. At that time even the Palestinian Pharisees actively propagated the faith of Israel among the heathen (Mt 23.15). Should the men of the primitive church join this chase after proselytes in order then to proclaim Jesus to them as the Christ? Jesus had after all taught no new religion, but as the bringer of eschatological salvation had fulfilled the old covenant in the new. Only as the fulfillment and abolition of the old covenant by a new one can the message of Jesus the Christ be proclaimed consistent with its actual nature. If there were to be an equally consistent mission to the heathen there would therefore first have to be the unification of the Old Testament message and the message of Jesus into a new doctrinal unity.

2. *Problems in the Development of Gentile Christianity Free from the Law*

Actually Gentile Christianity arose before the beginning of any actual mission to the heathen. According to the report of Acts it did not begin as a result of a congregational resolution or some leader's trail-blazing decisions, but as it were simply on its own, resulting from the dynamics of the gospel itself, i.e., it began by an act of God. *In Antioch*, the Hellenistic metropolis in Syria, unknown Christians (originally Diaspora Jews from Cyprus and Cyrene who had

110

fled from Jerusalem during the persecution which arose over Stephen) addressed their preaching about Jesus directly to the Hellenistic populace (Acts 11.20f.). And there arose a congregation of the uncircumcised who believed in Jesus as the bringer of all salvation, the first Gentile Christian congregation (Acts 11.19-21). The same process may shortly thereafter have been repeated in many other places. Luke refers only to Antioch because it became the first center of Gentile Christianity and because it was at Antioch that the special problems of Gentile Christianity arose and were solved.

The difference between the Christians in Jerusalem and those in Antioch was expressed by older historical criticism as the contrast between the law-abiding Jewish narrowness of the primitive Jerusalem congregation and Pauline universalism. The *Religionsgeschichliche Schule*, on the other hand, rightly introduced the comprehensive distinction between Palestinian and *Hellenistic Christianity*, Paul being an exponent only of the latter.[1] They maintain that Hellenistic Christianity, compared with the Palestinian, was a completely new expression of Christianity that arose from the distinctive presuppositions of the Hellenistic way of thinking. This distinction is weakened somewhat by the insight that Jewish and Hellenistic factors overlapped especially in the geographical area where Christianity arose; but it is an indispensable phenomenological datum. However, it still does not get at the real problem. Christianity's path from Jerusalem to Antioch was not only its first historical transfer from one cultural environment to another, but it was a decisive new departure in redemptive history, a *departure out of* the confining sphere of the *Old Testament Law*. This statement in no way implies a return to the above-

[1] Initially by W. Heitmüller, "Zum Problem Paulus und Jesus," *ZNW*, XIII (1912), 320-37, and W. Bousset, *Kyrios Christos* (Göttingen, 1913; 2d ed., 1921), pp. 75-104.

111

mentioned view, still represented by H. Lietzmann,[2] that between Jerusalem and Antioch stood only the problem of ritual law, a view which Luke's presentation seems to allow.

The true character of the problem about the Law which stood between Jerusalem and Antioch becomes clear in a consideration of the *internal problems of Gentile Christianity*. What sort of kerygma did the law-free Gentile Christians in Antioch have? Against a background of traditional Hellenistic ideas, their kerygma most likely united the vaguely abbreviated contents of the Old Testament with a message of Jesus the Savior no longer very clear because it was severed from its Old Testament presuppositions. The writings of the apostolic fathers, as a type, show what sort of kerygma may arise from these elements. Bultmann (*Theol.* 9-15) has been the first to try to reconstruct a total picture of the Hellenistic church's kerygma. He reconstructs it from those elements which the apostolic fathers, the general writings of the New Testament, and the Pauline letters presuppose to be universally accepted. His picture remains an abstract reconstruction which pulls together into one level things which were widely separated in point of time and of space. Perhaps it would be more consistent with the historical realities simply to present the problems and let the concrete answers remain in their historical place. What then was the crucial problem in Hellenistic Christianity? It was not the question which phenomenologically seems most urgent, concerning a Hellenistic substrata interspersing Palestinian tradition with new ideas and forms of expression. It is instead the *relationship of the message of Christ to the Old Testament*.

But precisely this question was at the same time the key problem for the Jerusalem Christians. Although raised by the crisis caused by Stephen, it was as yet unsolved. In

[2] H. Leitzmann, *History of the Early Church*, Vol. I, *The Beginnings of the Early Church* (4th ed.; New York, 1961), p. 107.

the Jerusalem congregation the clarification of this problem, Jesus and the Old Testament, became increasingly crucial for their relationship with Judaism.

Thus finally the problem about the Law which arose between Antioch and Jerusalem recalled both congregations to this most crucial and fundamental question of their whole existence, which neither of them had yet clarified. The message of Jesus still had to be properly related to the Old Testament and vice versa before the church could have its own genuine kerygma and be guarded against any undermining by Judaism or Hellenism. Until this problem found a solution that was consistent with the theological realities involved, the Christians were not safe from sinking back into either Judaism or syncretism. But with such a solution both congregations were led under the aegis of the genuine kerygma to churchly unity.

Not theoretical considerations, but God's redemptive handiwork itself, which had created a church both inside and outside Judaism, pressed for a *solution of this vital question*. Therefore it is entirely in keeping with the actual situation when we do not find any cross-section summary of the Hellenistic church's kerygma in the New Testament, but only the authoritative, apostolic formulation of the message to them, namely, *the Pauline epistles*. The solution of the problem we have been discussing constitutes the core of these epistles. Each of the two congregations is led in its own way to accept this solution.

3. *The Jerusalem Congregation Is Led into Fellowship with the Law-Free Gentile Church*

The book of *Acts* sees decisive elements of the problem in this hour of the church with astonishing clarity. It reports only briefly on the beginnings of Gentile missions, but describes very thoroughly how the *Jerusalem congregation was led* step by step *toward a recognition of Gentile Chris-*

113

tians in their freedom from the Law. The church in Jerusalem was continually being confronted with examples of Christian faith arising outside the boundaries of Judaism. In obedience to its responsibility for the brethren, it could not overlook such things; it had to test again and again[3] and acknowledge that what had happened was the redemptive work of God. When the church acknowledged as brethren those *Samaritans* baptized by Philip, it had not yet overcome its basic scruples, since the Samaritans did hold to the Pentateuch; but at least it had forsaken its deeply rooted nationalistic prejudices (Jn 4.9). Thus when the Samaritans received the extraordinary gift of the Spirit, it was for them and for Jerusalem Christians a confirmatory sign from God (Acts 8.14-17).[4] Philip's encounter with the *eunuch* and above all Peter's encounter with *Cornelius* led even further. Philip was unable to deny baptism to the eunuch who believed in Christ, though he could no longer be circumcised (Acts 8.36). Peter, though his conscience was much more strongly bound to the Law (Acts 10.14), could not refuse to baptize the uncircumcised Cornelius since God had given him his Spirit (Acts 10.47); and the Jerusalem church had to give silent acknowledgment. "If then God gave the same gift to them as he gave to us . . . , who was I that I could withstand God?" (Acts 11.17f.). This is how the church is created! What Peter and the Jerusalem church had done in the isolated case of Cornelius, Barnabas could not subsequently refuse to do in *Antioch* whither he was sent at the news of the establishment of a Gentile Christian church there. He could only joyfully acknowledge God's redemp-

[3] This testing did not imply that Christian Jerusalem sought to make the claim to primacy which Jewish Jerusalem did.

[4] The episode leaves many questions unanswered about the theology and history of this tradition. In any case Luke wants to report an extraordinary intervention of the Spirit. He does not seek to develop a general doctrine of the Spirit or of the special authority of the apostles. Viewed historically it may have been that this combination produced the first instance of Christians' eschatologically "extolling God" (Acts 10.46).

114

tive deed and, in addition, obediently recognize this as his field for further work (Acts 11.23). In all this, however, it was only individual cases of God's redemptive work that were being acknowledged, but as Acts reports and as the historical sequence especially shows, there was not yet any acknowledgment in principle of a Law-free gospel for Law-free Gentile Christians.[5] Before this could happen, the above-mentioned theological problem inherent in this Law-free Gentile Christianity, that is, where the Old Testament fits in, first had to be solved. Called to this theological task (this is underplayed in Acts) was that man whom Barnabas now brought to Antioch to work in the mother congregation of Gentile Christianity (Acts 11.25f.), Paul the apostle of Jesus Christ to the Gentiles.

[5] Historical criticism has long raised the following objections to the presentation of this epoch in Acts: The Cornelius episode as reported in Acts anticipates something that was not achieved until Paul's forceful persuasion at the apostolic council. Since Peter was the one who later in Antioch broke off table fellowship with the Gentile Christians (Gal 2.11ff.), he can hardly be the one who took the epochmaking step toward Cornelius. M. Dibelius in his Studies in the Acts of the Apostles (London, 1957) concludes that behind the Cornelius episode there is historically the "insignificant" conversion of a God-fearer by Peter. Luke then becomes the one who built it up to "fundamental significance" and with it justified the decision of the apostolic council (Acts 15.6-21). Gal 2 is actually the only historical account of the apostolic council.

This criticism of Acts goes much too far. Luke did abbreviate the historical development, but only in the following fashion: (1) He does not recognize that the Law-free gospel must first be formulated. Instead he thinks that the only thing necessary is to abolish the ceremonial law for the Gentile Christians and to maintain the gospel against the Judaizers. As a result, Paul's significance is underplayed, and the conversion of Cornelius overemphasized. (2) As Luke sees it there was one decisive intellectual breakthrough that conclusively annulled the ceremonial law for the Gentiles (Acts 10.9-16, 28; 11.2f.; 15.1, 19f.). In reality this matter remained a decision of conscience for Jewish Christians. So Peter could have his doubts in Antioch (Gal 2) whether table fellowship with the Gentiles really was allowed. But this is in no way contradicted when Peter on the basis of a particular experience baptizes the uncircumcised Cornelius and has fellowship with him. The men of Jerusalem would not have been moved to acknowledge the Law-free gospel by Paul's persuasion alone, if they themselves had not also experienced something decisive along this line.

4. Paul Settles the Internal Question

Paul[6] had created neither Gentile missions nor Gentile Christianity's freedom from the Law. He was neither the first nor the only missionary to the Gentiles, but he was *the Gentiles' apostle*. Not by expanding upon apostolic tradition, but rather by virtue of his own encounter with the crucified Christ as the resurrected One (Gal 1.1, 11f., 15ff.), Paul shaped the fundamental contours of the apostolic gospel for the Gentile church and therewith for the church as a whole (Gal 1.6).

His *provenance* and *development* had uniquely prepared him for his calling. His Hellenistic home town and the Judaism of the Diaspora had opened his eyes to the situation of the Hellenistic world and had given him the means for expressing himself intelligibly to it. His strictly pious home (Phil 3.4f.; Rom 11.1; 2 Cor 11.22) and his indoctrination in Pharisaic scribal learning had rooted him firmly in Judaism. Zealous for the law, he had become a persecutor of the church (Gal 1.13f.; Phil 3.5f.). Thus his experience at Damascus meant the most revolutionary change imaginable. Faith here did not rescue him from searching doubts and racking confusion (this was not his problem), but from his unequivocal rejection of Christ and his autocratic self-righteousness (Phil 3.6).[7] His past and his present now confronted each other as radical opposites. His past, how-

---

[6] C. G. Montefiore, *Judaism and St. Paul* (London, 1914). J. Knox, *St. Paul and the Church of Jerusalem* (Cambridge, 1930). J. Knox, *St. Paul and the Church of the Gentiles* (Cambridge, 1939, 1961). W. C. van Unnik, *Tarsus or Jerusalem?* (London, 1962). H. Windisch, *Paulus und das Judentum* (Stuttgart, 1935). W. D. Davies, *Paul and Rabbinic Judaism* (London, 1948). M. Dibelius and W. G. Kümmel, *Paul* (Philadelphia, 1953). A. M. Hunter, *Paul and His Predecessors* (London, 1961). H. J. Schoeps, *Paul. The Theology of the Apostle in the Light of Jewish Religious History* (London, 1961).

[7] The Damascus experience was not the product of a psychological development! Rom 7.7-25 is not to be understood biographically (see p. 139). Acts 26.14 speaks of the "goad" which now turns Paul into another path.

ever, was simply Jewish existence per se; Pharisaic scribalism was Judaism par excellence. Thus redemption by way of the Law and faith in the crucified Christ were for him mutually exclusive opposites. This became the hallmark of his apostolic work; little wonder, since he was called to faith and to the apostolate at the same time. In essence then, the event at Damascus was for him the same as the Easter experiences were for the original apostles (1 Cor 15.8ff.; 9.1).

Consciously appropriating the universalism of Old Testament prophecy (Gal 1.15-Jer 1.5; Is 49.1), he saw from the very beginning that he was called as *apostle to the nations* of the world. But, like the men of the Jerusalem church, he did not go to the metropolitan centers to make propaganda out on the streets for a new religion; he, too, *turned first of all to the synagogues* wherever he went. The synagogue for him was not just a tactical point of connection nor simply an interim stage of history, but rather a point of departure in redemptive history (Rom 1.16). In contrast to the men of the Jerusalem church, however, he and the congregations which gathered around his proclamation were *always immediately cast out of the synagogues* and thus directly forced into Gentile missions. The different reception granted him must stem *from the nature of his proclamation*.

More details can be inferred from the thorough report in Acts on the events in the synagogue at Antioch in Pisidia. When Paul preached there in the synagogue for the second time, almost the entire city gathered to hear him. "But when the Jews saw the multitudes, they were filled with jealousy, and contradicted . . . and reviled him" (Acts 13.45). The reason for this hateful jealousy is no longer quite clear from Luke's portrayal. It was not the great success Paul had as such. This could have aroused at the most only the envy of certain propagandists for Judaism. Jealousy flared up because *Paul bypassed Judaism in offering salvation to the*

117

Gentiles. His proclamation awakened in the "God-fearers" and the Gentiles who were present the question of the jailer of Philippi, and Paul could never answer with anything but, "Believe in the Lord Jesus, and you will be saved, you and your household" (Acts 16.31). This faith alone, without circumcision and without subjection to the Law, granted a share in the messianic salvation, that salvation which Israel and its proselytes hoped to attain by reason of their faithfulness to the Law. If this were true, then the fundamental claim of the synagogue and the basis of Judaism's whole religious and national existence, namely, that circumcision and fulfilling of the Law were prerequisites for attaining salvation, was declared void—not from a more liberal viewpoint, but from the perspective of redemptive history itself. Thus *began the most thoroughgoing change in the history of Judaism*. The Gentiles who had previously been attracted to the synagogue, and many others besides, now gathered together into a congregation which believed in Jesus as the promised One of Israel. But the broad masses of the synagogue as such rejected this faith and were themselves left behind, isolated in their negation and outlawed as the disobedient, obstinate nation. In encountering Paul's proclamation, the one people who had testified of God's coming salvation to all peoples transformed itself into post-Christian Judaism, isolating itself in its opposition, clinging to the Law instead of the gospel and persecuting the church. With the Gentile church arising in this way, Paul now brought the proclamation which was expelled from the synagogue directly to the Gentiles. Since the synagogue sensed its own condemnation in the existence and proclamation of this church, it tried to suppress them both (1 Thess 2.15f.). It persecuted Paul with bitter hatred to the very end as the man whose proclamation destroyed its previous position among the nations of the world and thus denied its very reason for existence.

In Paul's preaching the Old Testament and the message of Jesus were authoritatively combined into a new unity, namely, *the gospel free from the Law*. Now God's salvation could fill out the pattern previously traced both by redemptive history and by the promise. It could make its way to the nations of the world as on every hand "to the Jew first and also to the Greek" this one gospel was being offered as "the power of God for salvation" (Rom 1.16). By rejecting the gospel, Israel was passing it on to the nations, not positively but negatively, and thus writing the conclusion to the revolutionary upheaval in redemptive history which had taken place on the cross. However, the task of explicating and defending this Law-free gospel was the distinctive apostolic service rendered by Paul.

5. *The Apostolic Council: Uniting Jews and Gentiles into the Church Distinct from Judaism*

It was this foundation of the Gentile church (actually, the foundation of the church as a whole) just sketched above which was at stake (Gal 2.2) when *Jewish Christians from Jerusalem* came to Antioch demanding that the Gentile Christians be circumcised and subjected to the Law as a prerequisite for salvation (Acts 15.1,5; Gal 2.3f.). Perhaps the events of the first missionary journey had also aroused the Jews in Jerusalem and incited them to reproach the Jerusalem Christians. But whatever the cause may have been, further development of Gentile Christianity free from the Law forced the Jerusalem church to re-appraise its own stand on the Law and at first gave rise to the *Judaizing tendency*. The demand reported in Acts 15.1 was a classic expression of the Judaizers' program. They could appeal to the practice of the Jerusalem congregation. This congregation preserved the tradition of Jesus' earthly ministry. It was the seat of the original apostles. This lent weight to their words and *necessitated a fundamental clarification of this question in Jerusalem* itself between the representatives of Gentile Christianity and Jewish Christianity.

At first there was strong opposition in the Jerusalem congregation (Gal 2.5; Acts 15.5,7) against acknowledging the Law-free gospel which Paul proclaimed so emphatically before the *apostolic council.* The existence and effectiveness of the Jerusalem congregation within Judaism were at stake. Their consciences, bound to former practice, bristled. But finally their representatives had to *acknowledge the Law-free gospel* if they did not wish to deny that from the very beginning Christ had established them also on faith alone.[8] The men of Jerusalem confessed that they were doing the same work as Paul and Barnabas in the service of the same gospel, only that the form of their service was different since they carried it out among the Jews and Paul and Barnabas among the Gentiles (Gal 2.9).

This *decision had* far-reaching *consequences.* All the participants thus confessed that they were members of the one church and with this confession they continued to be such. Palestinian Jewish Christianity did not slip back into Judaism, but rather continued to lend its strength to Gentile Christianity. Gentile Christianity, however, remained connected with the current of tradition from Jesus' earthly life and its Old Testament background, and retained therein its most powerful defense against being sucked into syncretism. The men of Jerusalem continued to carry the "spiritual blessings" (Rom 15.27) of the first congregation into the Gentile church, and the representatives of the Gentile church acknowledged their connection with the little group of Jesus' witnesses still holding out in Israel by taking up a collection for them (Gal. 2.10). Except for some

[8] The apostolic decree of Acts 15.19f., 28f. was probably not promulgated until later, after the incident in Antioch (Gal 2.11-14). In Acts 21.25 James passes it on to Paul. By no means does it intend to limit freedom from the law (cf. Chap. X, note 4).

peripheral incidents the split between Jewish and Hellenistic Christianity that threatened the church, beginning with the persecution which arose over Stephen, amounted to only an interlude for the whole church in New Testament times, as far as the heart of the kerygma was concerned. A formal unity of teaching or even of a way of life never resulted, but there was a basic acknowledgment of the living truth of the apostolic message in both places, which gave free rein to the message and made the unity of the church a reality. Believing Jews and believing Gentiles confessed themselves to be the redemptive community of the last days, transcending both Jews and Gentiles. The whole church broke through the shell of Judaism and set about even externally to become what Christ had intended it to be, the church of God made up of all peoples. The complete removal of this shell, however, still required bitter struggle.

Chapter X

The Church Separated from Judaism

According to the *simplified presentation in* Acts the apostolic council was the final victorious solution of the internal problems: the question of table fellowship was solved by the story of Cornelius, and the Judaizers were averted; in a quick march of victory Paul now gathered the rapidly growing churches made up chiefly of Gentiles, and in every place tore them away from the synagogues. *Paul's letters*, however, bear witness to the continual flare-up of the inner struggle to separate from Judaism. Ultimate separation was for the most part actually accomplished simply by the overwhelming weight of Gentile Christianity. The service rendered by Paul was that it was accomplished for theologically valid reasons so as to set a standard for the future.

1. *The Duty of Jewish Christianity Toward the Law Is Not Yet Clarified*

The *difficulties* which still remained after the Jerusalem decision *broke out in the episode at* Antioch (Gal 2.11-21). The Jerusalem decision acknowledged a basic Koinonia (participating, sharing fellowship, Acts 2.42) between circumcised and uncircumcised believers. This could easily be granted to the uncircumcised Titus in Jerusalem, where everything was ordered according to the Law anyway (Gal 2.3). But how should the Jewish Christian minorities in Gentile Christian congregations behave? *Could these Jewish Christians* now be allowed to ignore the Law as well and *have table fellowship with the Gentile Christians?* Leading men in the church, as the episode in Antioch shows, took a position toward this problem which cast doubt on the enforcement of the Jerusalem decision.

Shortly after the apostolic council *Peter came to Anti-*

och. At the congregational meals (1 Cor 11.20ff.) he had joined in the table fellowship between Jews and Gentiles, where from the very beginning they had probably practiced paying no attention to the laws of purity. God's work among the Gentiles, which Peter had fundamentally acknowledged in Jerusalem, also cast its spell on him, as it had previously done to Barnabas and other men of the Jerusalem church. Then messengers appeared from the Lord's brother, James, the leader of the Jerusalem church (Gal 2.9; Acts 12.17; 21.18), and probably on commission from him, or at least with his consent (cf. Acts 21.18ff.), they raised this objection (Gal 2.12): Certainly the Gentile Christians should not be burdened with the Law, but this did not mean that Jewish Christians might discard it. Even if they placed their confidence for salvation in Christ alone, they should not be allowed to stop living like pious Jews. Thereupon Peter, along with the other Jewish Christians, even Barnabas, broke off table fellowship with the Gentile Christians. This probably also applied to the Lord's Supper, which was woven directly into the general congregational meal. The authority of Peter and that of James, and the power of Jewish tradition, became evident.

During this time *Paul* was probably temporarily absent. His recorded reaction presupposes that the separation had already taken place. He called Peter to account before the assembled congregation. Paul did not repudiate the keeping of the Mosaic ordinances by Jewish Christians as such, nor the practice of the Jerusalem church. If Peter had held back because of conscience scruples, without reprimanding anyone else, Paul probably would have condoned his action somewhat in the sense of Rom 14.1ff., little as he could consent to the objection of the James faction. But in all severity Paul objected to the fact that Peter had abandoned his original position he had taken in faith toward Christ. Thus Peter had given the impression that faith in Christ had led him to sin (Gal 2.17f.), and that the believers, even the

Gentile Christians, contrary to the Jerusalem decision (Gal 2.14), were still under obligation to keep the Law (Gal 2.19; cf. 15f.).

Paul was still in harmony not only with Peter, but also with James (cf. Acts 21.18ff.), in the basic article that only faith in Christ works salvation (Gal 2.15f.), and that therefore the Gentiles should not be burdened with the Law. But whereas Paul concluded from this that no believer in Christ, not even a Jewish Christian, was under obligation to keep the Law any more, James was unwilling to draw this conclusion for Jewish Christians. Peter wavered between both positions; but from that time on, as can be inferred from his further career, he moved in the direction of Paul's position.[1]

It was clear to anyone who cast a glance to the future that the halfway solution of James could not be maintained permanently. What Peter had done today could be expected tomorrow from every Jewish Christian in the Diaspora. Acknowledging Gentile Christianity's freedom from the Law had to lead to the same freedom for the Jewish Christian minorities in Gentile Christian congregations. The attempt was made to prevent this at all costs in Palestinian Christianity, for the consequences would be far-reaching (Acts 21.20ff.). Thus the incident in Antioch may have given new impetus to the Judaizers, whose views had been rejected at the apostolic council.

2. *The Final Rejection of Judaizing in the Gentile Church (Galatians)*

After the apostolic council Paul once more had to take up the *fight against Judaizing* teachers from Palestine who

---

[1] Opposed to this view is the opinion of H. Lietzmann, (Chap. IX, note 2) I, 108, 151f., that because of this incident Peter forsook the decision of the apostolic council and organized a Judaizing countermission against Paul. This conjecture contradicts all subsequent reports about Peter. See O. Cullmann, *Peter: Disciple, Apostle, Martyr* (1st ed.; Philadelphia, 1953; 2d ed., 1962).

this time sought to heal the breach between Christianity and Judaism in his field of labor by demanding that the Gentile Christians submit to the Law. The document which remains from this conflict is the letter to the Galatians.

The *churches of Galatia* were being "troubled" by the proclamation of a "gospel" which was "different" from that of Paul (Gal 1.6-9). Circumcision was demanded (Gal 5.3, 12; 6.12,15; cf. 2.3f.) of the Galatians, the majority of whom were Gentile Christians (Gal 4.8f.). It was demanded as a sign that they acknowledged the Law (Gal 4.21), at least its basic features (Gal 5.3) which also included keeping the Mosaic festivals, particularly the Sabbath (Gal 4.10). It was also to be a sign that they belonged to the seed of Abraham, to the people of God who were heirs to the promise (Gal 3.6-16; 29; 6.16). This recognition of the Law was not supposed to supplant faith in Christ; obedience to the Law, the "work of the Law" was rather the necessary extension and perfecting of faith in Christ (Gal 3.2-5). Not until they had acknowledged this did the believers become members of the redeemed nation! Did not the promises in scripture apply to the circumcised nation? Only when this call to acknowledge the Law is combined with faith in Christ, does one have the whole gospel (Gal 1.7) as it was represented by the original apostles. Paul, after all, was not directly an apostle of Jesus; in appropriating his proclamation from the original apostles he had not received their total message (Gal 1.11f., 18f.).[2] The

[2] In the Jewish Christian document *Kerygmata Petru* of about 170 Peter says the following against Paul (Ps-Clem. *Hom.* 17, 19): "If Jesus made himself known to you through visions, this is a sign of his wrath. How could anyone be instructed by a vision to qualify for the teaching office? And if you object that it is possible, then why did our master associate with us for a whole year in our waking hours? . . . And how could he possibly have appeared to you since you think exactly the opposite of his teaching? . . . If you really wish to become a co-worker for the truth, then learn first from us what we have learned from Jesus, and then as a disciple of the truth become our co-worker." In this and similar fashion Paul was already being attacked again and again by Judaizers while he was still alive.

spokesmen for this teaching which troubled the churches of Galatia (Gal 1.7; 5.10) were in every way like the "false brethren" in Antioch (Gal 2.4f.; Acts 15.1,5); like them, they were nomistic Judiazers from Palestine.

This teaching exercised *an astonishing pull* on the Galatian Gentile Christians. They followed it as if seized by some magic (Gal 3.1; cf. 1.6). The teaching appeared to be a harmless finishing touch to the Pauline proclamation. It afforded the Gentiles the much-sought-after connection with an ancient religion which in addition gave them the protection of a *religio licita* (a religion legally tolerated by the Roman government), and spared the Jewish Christians the painful conflict with their fellow Jews (Gal 5.11; 6.12).

Paul uncovers the *heart of the matter*: both the seducer and the seduced were fleeing from the cross of Christ. The cross of Christ meant an absolute break with Judaism as well as with the world (Gal 6.14f.). Through the cross the believer knows that he is "crucified" to the world and to the Law (Gal 2.19f.; 6.14). Accepting the Law therefore meant not perfecting the new, but relapsing into the old, yes, even being on the level of heathenism (Gal 4.8f.; cf. 3.3); for life under the Law, like heathenism, basically meant being subject to elemental spirits. The "different gospel" therefore was in reality no gospel (Gal 1.7). According to that gospel Jesus was only one stone in the old edifice of Judaism, but for Paul He was the cornerstone of a new building (Gal 4.21-31). There remained only the either-or possibility: either Christ or the Law.

The letter to the *Galatians is the only letter* in which *Paul reacts* to an attempt *to subject the church to the Law*. There is no mention of this in the Corinthian letters, nor in the letters to the Philippians and the Romans. That is why the polemic statements in Phil 3.2f. (18f.) and Rom 16.17-20, ambiguous in their brevity, can hardly be directed against nomistic Judaizers. The Judaizers who were dismissed by the letter to the Galatians (1 Cor 16.1) may have

126

continued to try winning individuals here and there in the Gentile Christian congregations for their cause, but their cause as such had already become *hopeless* by the time of the letter to the Corinthians. The idea promulgated by exegetes of the Tübingen school in the nineteenth century, and still persisting, that a competitive nomistic Judaizing mission arose in Paul's whole mission area and for a time split it into two camps is completely erroneous. Already at the time of the letters to the Corinthians, Paul no longer had to defend Gentile Christianity's freedom from the Law against nomistic Judaizing, but instead he had to protect conscience-bound Jewish Christians against Gentile Christians, and warn the latter against a completely different type of Judaizing seduction.

3. *The Jewish Christians as "Weak Brethren"*

In Corinth the majority of the congregation, on the basis of their "knowledge," ate food offered to idols with no qualms (1 Cor 8.1,10). Several, however, were offended at this; "because of their consciousness that idols are involved" they "eat food as really offered to an idol; and their conscience, being weak, is defiled" (1 Cor 8.7). The consciousness of idols which Paul envisions here was the shyness toward idols drilled into the conscience of the Jew, not the Gentile's familiarity with them. The original word, *eidolothyton,* is the Jewish word for meat coming from a heathen offering, which the Gentiles called by a different Greek word, *ierothyton* (1 Cor 10.28). Eating this was strictly forbidden to the Jews; for a Gentile Christian to observe this abstinence, though it was of no real concern to him, would have meant his exclusion from all sociability. The "weak," of whom the "strong" were to be considerate in love (1 Cor 8.9-13; 10.28ff.; cf. 9.19-23), therefore, were congregation members who were bound by the traditions of Law-abiding Judaism.

This interpretation of the situation in Corinth is confirmed by the character of a similar movement in Rome. In the congregation at Rome a minority avoided eating meat and drinking wine (Rom 14.2,21) and observed particular days (Rom 14.5). Ascetic currents were widespread in the world of that time; but the combination of this sort of demand with Paul's acknowledgment of it as a genuine qualm of conscience is most simply explained if it has to do with the after-effects of Jewish customs. Abstention from meat and wine, to be sure, was not commanded generally anywhere in the Law, but in the Diaspora it was widely practiced simply for the sake of the first commandment, for there the Jew always had to fear that meat and wine had been used in connection with sacrificial ceremonies and thus had become "common" (Rom 14.4; cf. Acts 10.15).[3] Observing particular days is easily explained as the after-effects of the Diaspora Jews' sanctifying the feast days, especially the Sabbath, as an act of confession. Here, too, the "weak" were therefore probably Christians who were still bound to Jewish traditions. Christ's exclusive redemptive mediation was apparently not questioned; therefore Paul admonished the "strong," who had become completely free in faith, to be considerate of the weak for the sake of love. For their part, however, the weak were not to judge the others (Rom 14.3f.,13,15; 15.1).[4]

[3] In this regard Daniel was the model of a Jew living among the heathen, according to Dan 1.8-16.

[4] The same purpose is served by the apostolic decree in Acts 15.28f. (see Chap. IX, note 8) as by Paul's admonitions in 1 Cor 8-10 and Rom 14f. It pledges the Gentile Christians to abstain from foods containing blood, especially non-kosher meat, from meat offered to idols, and from marital union within certain degrees of family relationships. These foods and these actions according to Lev 17f. were ever forbidden for the stranger living in Israel. As a sign of heathen impurity they were a gross offense to every Jew. Gentile Christians were admonished to abstain from them in order to make it easier for Jewish Christians still bound by their conscience scruples to have table fellowship with them. In the post-Pauline era keeping these rules became an act of confession against gnostic libertinism (Rev 2.14,20). In the second century the regulation was also understood in a transferred sense: the "strangled" reference was bypassed and the remaining injunctions transferred to the three mortal sins: idolatry,

Thus only a few years after the apostolic council the relationship between Gentile and Jewish Christians had fundamentally changed. Before that the Jewish Christians were admonished to give full recognition to the Gentile Christians; now the Gentile Christians had to be admonished to consider the Jewish Christians as brethren. The *Jewish Christians in the Gentile Christian congregations* who were still bound in their consciences to the Jewish traditions *had become* "weak," namely, weak in faith (Rom 14.1), lacking the knowledge of the full Christians (1 Cor 8.7) and thus not yet completely released from their pre-Christian past. Should they not have endeavored to overcome this "weakness," to let their pre-Christian ties go completely by the board? This was indeed the case.

4. *The Final Separation from Judaism in the Greek and in the Palestinian Churches*

When Paul came to Jerusalem with the collection after finishing his great missionary journey in the Orient, in order to set out from there for the west, some people in the Jerusalem church raised an objection against him: that he taught "all the Jews [Jewish Christians] who are among the Gentiles [Gentile Christians] to forsake Moses, telling them not to circumcise their children or observe the customs" (Acts 21.21). Thus *the Jewish Christians in the Gentile Christian congregations were ceasing to live according to the Mosaic ordinances;* they were separating themselves completely from Judaism and were being absorbed into Gentile Christian congregations. In the Jerusalem congregation some maintained that Paul was the cause of this. James asked him to clear himself from this suspicion by proving his own respect for the Law (Acts 21.24), and according to Acts (21.26) Paul conceded. Actually Paul had never forced Jewish Christians to give up their inherited

---

murder, and fornication, and then expanded with the golden rule (thus the Western textual tradition).

customs, but had rather admonished the Gentile Christians to give them due consideration. But neither had he obligated them to maintain the Law, as James did. On the contrary he had given them complete freedom. This contrast with James is concealed by Acts.

Although this process within Jewish Christianity disturbed the Jerusalem congregation, it could not be stopped. It came to a conclusion for the most part during the era of Paul's ministry. After A.D. 70 Jewish Christian minorities living according to Jewish customs were not to be found in the Greek church between Ephesus and Rome. Only in Syria and in Egypt did this separation from Judaism take longer. With the extinction of Jewish Christianity living according to Jewish customs in the midst of Gentile congregations, the Gentile church lost its last outward tie with Judaism.

Even before this separation from Judaism was completed in the Greek church, the ties between Judaism and Christianity were also cut in Palestine, at least outwardly. In the year 62 when Festus, the Roman governor known from the story of Paul, left office prematurely and his successor Albinus had not yet arrived, Hannas, the high priest, used this interim to do away with persons under his displeasure, including the Lord's brother, James.[5] The murder of this leader of the Jerusalem church, who was known by Jews and Christians alike as "the Righteous" because of his faithfulness to the Law, was a sign of the final break,[6] even apart from the particular circumstances which are no longer quite clear. In the year 66 when the Zealots came to power

[5] Thus, according to Josephus, Ant., 20,9,1; cf. Eusebius, Hist. Eccl. 2.23. According to Hegesippus' legendary report (Eusebius, Hist. Eccl. 2.23.11-18) James was cast from the Temple pinnacle by the Pharisees and scribes shortly before the Jewish revolt.

[6] James had to the very end daily prayed in the Temple for the conversion of Israel (Hegesippus' report in Eusebius, Hist. Eccl. 2.23.6f.). When he was finally expelled from the Temple, the Jerusalem church most likely also left the Temple for good.

130

and Roman rule collapsed, the "Nazarenes" (i.e., Christian Jews) were the only group in the Jewish nation which clearly withdrew from the zealotic delusion.[7] As a result they had to flee from the fanaticism which persecuted them as traitors and deserters. In the Jewish folk-community which gathered anew after the catastrophe there was no longer any room for these "Nazarenes."

The church therewith became externally what it had already confessed itself to be internally at the apostolic council, namely, a fellowship of Jews and Gentiles distinct from Judaism. The redeemed community had at first stood distinct from Israel as the latter still waited for God's salvation. Now it stood opposite the Jews as they rejected God's salvation (cf. Acts 28.17-28). Thus the relationship between Christianity and Judaism and at the same time the church itself had achieved the form which would characterize them down through the centuries. It is completely consonant that Luke should conclude his report of the formation of the church at this very hour.

The original impetus for such development in the relationship between Christianity and Judaism lay in the nature of Jesus' own earthly ministry. He abolished the redemptive mediation of the Law and offered Himself instead in fellowship. In His signs He granted eschatological redemptive fellowship with God to that faith which sought salvation only through Him.

This fellowship was the goal of his entire call to repentance: it was participation in the kingdom of God. Thus Jesus proclaimed the message of the coming of God's kingdom and at the same time He initiated its arrival concealed in the activity of His life and ministry.

How does one evaluate the subsequent development that arose from this initial impetus? The first kerygma pro-

[7] All Jewish groups, including the Essenes, participated in the revolt (Josephus, Bell., 2,8,10; 2,20,4)!

131

claimed by the first apostles to their fellow Jews was conditioned by additional factors. These included Judaism's rejection of Jesus and God's salutary act of resurrecting Him coupled with Jesus' own self-revelation in the Easter appearances and His continued activity through the Spirit. These factors shaped the proclamation as follows: The crucified Jesus of Nazareth who had demanded complete obedience and granted complete forgiveness is the promised One of Israel; as the Son of man, now elevated to the right hand of God and through whom the spirit is working, He will soon appear in glory. By Paul's time there again were additional factors to be reckoned with: Israel's stubbornness had now also asserted itself against the apostolic kerygma, and God had initiated redemptive action among the Gentiles. So Paul by virtue of his call transposed the apostolic proclamation to Israel into the gospel for both Jews and Gentiles: Jesus was the promised one whose fulfilling of God's Old Testament order annuls it and brings about a new one. This was exactly what the historical Jesus Himself had claimed to be although hidden behind signs. This step-by-step formulation of the kerygma, which each time received an initial impulse from the attitude of Judaism, corresponds also to the formation of the church, the new people of God: The circle of the twelve is the hidden sign and blueprint of it; the Pentecost congregation is the actual pouring of its foundation; and the church under the Pauline gospel reveals its basic structural formation.

Certainly Israel's rejection of the gospel and the rise of a Gentile church were not the only factors that conditioned the shape of the gospel and the church. Certainly both Jewish and Hellenistic traditions also came to the church's assistance in expressing the kerygma and explicating its theology. It was, for example, by these means that the various conceptual languages arose by means of which the gospel was proclaimed: What the synoptic gospels call repentance, Paul calls dying together with Christ in order to

132

live together with Him, while for John it constitutes being born again. Certainly there are manifold instances where the gospel is applied to particular current situations. Paul himself is already doing this in virtually every epistle as he highlights a different facet of the gospel and applies new forms of expression. As a result there is great variety in individual details in the proclamation's course of development as well as in the structuring of the churches. The course of the development that we have sought to trace was *the main line,* and the events that affected this main line were the decisive factors. *The decisive factors* have proved to be not the influences of traditions nor the particular kerygmatic intentions of certain witnesses, but the reciprocal interaction between the message and an event brought about by God, an event which takes historical form as either faith or unfaith.

This view of the development agrees with the position expressed in *Romans.* Here Paul, after completing his work in the Oriental world and turning to the West, presents his gospel to the Roman congregation, a congregation as yet unknown to him. His gospel is the message of Jesus Christ (Rom 1.3f.), interpreted as the message of righteousness (Rom 1.16f.) by means of which Judaism with its existence under the Law is annulled (Rom 1-8), and which is also valid for an initially unbelieving Israel (Rom 9-11). Paul does not present his gospel in this fashion because the Roman congregation is particularly interested in such issues, but because in that crucial hour of separation between church and synagogue the entire church must hear the gospel precisely in this form. Since this *heilgeschichtlich* situation persists to this day, Romans remains for all times the central theological summary of the Pauline gospel, and thereby the *central theological summary of the entire apostolic gospel.* It unfolds the gospel by showing the meaning of the break between church and synagogue.

133

Chapter XI

Paul Interprets the Break: Judaism as a Sample of Pre-Christian Existence (Romans 1–8)

1. *The New Situation in Redemptive History*

As Paul prepared to deliver the offerings which the churches he founded around the Aegean Sea had gathered for the mother church in Jerusalem, he considered his missionary task in the eastern portion of the globe finished. His letter to the Romans written at this time says as much: The promised *advent of the message* of salvation in the end-time has become an accomplished fact for this part of the world (Rom 15.19-33; cf. Is 52.7; Rom 10.15). What were *the results?* The Gentile nations came in droves (Rom 9.25f.; 10.8ff.), but the vast majority of *Israel* both in the mother country as well as in the Diaspora *rejected the gospel* (Rom 9.1ff.; 27ff.; 11.7). Viewing history in the way the prophets did, Paul saw this historical reality to be a new constitutive factor in redemptive history. While James, the Lord's brother, still strove for the conversion of his people in the hope of changing the situation, Paul attempted in his letter to the Romans to interpret this outcome which actually was not changed by any further mission work. His view of the situation in redemptive history and his interpretation have found confirmation, insofar as this is possible, in the two thousand years of church history which have elapsed since then. The basically antithetical stance of church and synagogue reached at the end of the Pauline mission still persists today. Thus Christianity and Judaism have not developed a side-by-side relationship as two branch religions historically growing from the same stem. Instead their antithetical relationship, as Paul shows in his sum-

134

marizing presentation of the gospel that sustains the church, has remained an essential part of that very gospel. This is true in reference to *two facets* into which *the relationship* finally precipitates. These are apparent in Romans even in its very terminology. The terminology also indicates the fact that formerly these two facets were synonymous. Rom 1-8 speaks of "*Jews*,"[1] and Rom 9-11 of "*Israel.*"[2]

The meaning of this distinction is already disclosed by Paul's word usage apart from Romans. *The term "Jew"* means for him generally not only one who formally belongs to the Jewish folk-community, but also one who belongs to the practicing religious community. "Jew" is the man of Jewish blood bound to the Law. Since this is the essential hallmark of the Jew, Paul can no longer refer to himself as a Jew after his conversion without qualification; he is only a "Jew by birth" (Gal 2.15). He can become "as a Jew" to the Jews, namely, "to those under the law as one under the law—though not myself under the law" (1 Cor 9.20). However, even as a Christian he can still continue to call himself a "Hebrew" (Phil 3.5; 2 Cor 11.22) as a child of a Jewish-Palestinian family, and an "Israelite" (2 Cor 11.22; Rom 11.1; cf. Phil 3.5) as a member of the nation standing within God's covenant and called to God's salvation (Eph 2.12). In Romans this word usage is narrowed down to designate a specific type. Here the word "Jew" means the circumcised man under the Old Testament word of revelation which as Law lays on him greater responsibility than on others (Rom 2.9f.; cf. 3.9,29), but which also as word of promise blesses him above others (Rom 3.1f.; 1.16). However, finally the "Jew" is that man who actually is *subject to the Law*, so that the circumcised are only relatively

[1] Most often in the singular and without the article: Rom 1.16; 2.9f., 17,28f.; 3.1. In the plural only in 3.9 (29). Elsewhere, in Rom 9.24 and 10.12.

[2] Rom 9.6,27,31; 10.(1),19,21; 11.2,7,25f.; "Israelite" occurs in 9.4 and 11.1.

accurate when they "call themselves Jews" (Rom 2.17,28 f.; cf. Rev 2.9; 3.9). "*Israel,*" on the other hand, refers to the people whose existence as a *people* stands *under the promise* of the Old Testament revelation (Rom 9.4f.).

The themes which are treated in the first two sections of Romans correspond to this word usage. Rom 1-8 proclaims existence under the gospel in its connection with the pre-Christian relationship to God, of which the Jew is an example. Rom 9-11 clarifies the relationship of the Jewish people to the gospel and to the church even as they reject that gospel. Thus what we call "Judaism" appears in twofold form in Romans. First, the *attitude of* "*the Jew,*" which is exposed in the call to repentance of the prophets and of Jesus, is an *example of the attitude of the pre-Christian man* who is subjected to the Law, lives in conflict with it, and yet is marked with the promise. Second, the *historical path of the Jewish people*, to whom as God's people the covenant and promise are granted, and who nevertheless reject the promised One and wind up standing opposite the church, raises the whole question of the *certainty of salvation*. In these two forms Judaism remains "connected" with the gospel until the end of the world. In addition, there is the third point that God's gracious and judgmental action toward the fathers and toward Israel to which the Old Testament testifies is "typos," typifying God's action toward the church (Rom 4.23f.; 1 Cor 10.11).[3] But we do not refer to this *Old Testament Israel* as "Judaism."

2. *Pre-Christian Existence Under the Law*

"To the Jew first but also to the Greek," the gospel is deliverance from the judgment of wrath (Rom 1.16f.) to

[3] L. Goppelt, *Typos, Die typologische Deutung des Alten Testaments im Neuen* (Gütersloh, 1939). L. Goppelt, *Apokalyptik und Typologie bei paulus,* ThLZ 89 (1964). G. W. H. Lampe and K. J. W. Woollkombe, *Essays on Typology* (London, 1957).

which both are subject in their interaction with sin (Rom 1.18-3.20). In Paul's view the Jew is not merely one historical part of pre-Christian humanity, but its very summit, which demonstrates the depravity of all (Rom 2.5-10; 3.9). In a universal extension of the view Jesus held toward "sinners and righteous," Rom 1.18-2.16 describes both the amoral and the moral man, the first living in a relationship to God by nature, the second by retributive justice. The first denies without exception God's witness to himself in creation, although it is inescapable and thus eliminates every possible excuse. Consequently he falls into an amorality which decimates his own life. The second condemns this attitude on the basis of his confession of retributive justice, but thereby he also condemns himself, for he does the same (Rom 2.1).

This is demonstrated in Rom 2.17-29 with the moral man per se, the Jew. He knows God's will. He boasts in the Law and teaches it to others, but he himself does not fulfill it (cf. Gal 6.13). He transgresses the most elementary commandments of the second table: he commits robbery and adultery (Rom 2.21f.). Naturally Paul is not saying here that among the people under the Law as a whole this occasionally happens; the Pharisees had long ago drawn the consequences of this foregone conclusion. It is precisely the conscious representatives of the Law, the Pharisaic Rabbis, whom Paul accuses of this sin. He does not maintain that every one of them does all of this, but rather that the Jew does it although he boasts in the Law. Paul probably does not mean the robbery and adultery implied in Jesus' call to repentance based on the new commandment (the sins of the heart in the Sermon on the Mount, Mt 5.27f.), but rather he is thinking in the sense of Jesus' words based on the Law: the scribes of the Pharisees, who were lovers of money (Lk 16.14), "devour widow's houses" (Mk 12.40). They commit adultery with the help of a certificate of divorce (Mk 10.11f.). The Jew abhors the idols of the heathen, especially the worship of mammon and unchastity, and yet he grasps them greedily to himself: "You who abhor idols, you rob (their) temples" (Rom 2.22). Under the appearance of justice the Jew avoids God's commandment with the help of casuistic misuse of the Law in such a way that it actually remains undone. "You who boast in the Law, you dishonor God by breaking the Law!" (Rom 2.23; cf. Acts 7.53). The truth of the matter is that only that man is a Jew, a man under the Law, whose "circumcision is a matter of the heart," who with his whole heart is subject to God, spiritually and not literally (Rom 2.28f.). This *true Jew*, even according to the Old Testament, was not a historical reality, but a *prophecy*. How far the actual Jew was separated from this inner unity with the Law is fully shown in Rom 9.30-10.4 (see p. 153). The formal tone of this presentation already betrays the actual theological origin of this judgment and its standard. It is made as the negative side of the proclamation of the cross following Jesus' word of repentance and the prophetic predictions about the new heart (Ezek 36.26; Jer 31.33; 2 Cor 3.3,6ff.).

The Jew's addiction to sin proves *the addiction of everyone* (Rom 3.9), for the core content of *the Law* under which he is guilty *applies to all pre-Christian humanity.* Law for Paul always means the Mosaic Law,[4] but this Law is the embodiment of the demands and ordinances of God applying to all to the end of this world.[5] The *demand of*

---

[4] W. Gutbrod's article νόμος in *TWNT*, IV, 1061ff. This excellent article is also published as *Bible Key Words*, tr. and ed. by J. R. Coats, *Law* by H. Kleinknecht and W. Gutbrod (London 1962).

[5] Galatians, which speaks less in principle and more in view of the practical situation, initially makes a sharp distinction: The Mosaic Law as such is valid only for the circumcised, but for them it is totally valid (Gal 5.3). The Gentiles, however, are subject to the cosmic elements, who are conceived of as angelic beings (Gal 4.3,8f.), and to the elemental statutes that arise from the cosmic order (Col 2.20). But nevertheless, since the Law was mediated by angels, being under the Law or being under the cosmic elements intrinsically amounts to exactly the same thing (Gal 4.3ff., 8f.).

the Law reveals itself to the non-Jew only piecemeal in actu, but in such a way that the excuse of ignorance is entirely excluded (Rom 2.12-16). The ordinance of Law, the retribution according to works in time and eternity, stands directly over all men (Rom 2.5-11). The retributive principle is very well known (Rom 1.32). This Law, which is the embodiment of God's ordinance over the first creation, to which every man is subject by nature (Rom 7.1-6), does not effect man's union with God, but rather "knowledge of sin"; not salvation, but wrath (Rom 3.20; 4.15).

This general activity effected by the Law corresponds to its place in the history of humanity which Paul portrays in Rom 5.12-21. All humanity stands in the shadow of an original "no" to God's commandment. By virtue of Adam's fall God's judgment has given up all to sin and death (Rom 5.18). The Law could not and was not meant to turn the tide of this destruction, but rather to bring it to a head. It "came in, to increase the trespass" (Rom 5.20), to goad disobedience into transgression and to give it up to wrath (Rom 4.15; 5.13; cf. Gal 3.19).

The existential anthropological form which sin takes when brought to a head by the Law, and at the same time its general and constant significance for faith are apparent from Rom 7.7-25. Here Paul talks no longer about the encounter of the Jew with the Law, but rather confesses in the first person that the encounter of the Adamite man with the Law is essentially his own origin and that of all believers. Here he is not autobiographically describing his pre-Christian past. When he does engage in autobiography he expresses himself in keeping with the common terms for Jewish self-awareness[6] as in Phil 3.6. But here from the van-

[6] Pharisaic-rabbinic Judaism always emphasized that man had the freedom, the liberum arbitrium, to choose between the "good" and the "evil desire" in his heart. Even the pessimistic book of 4 Ez asserts this (TWNT, IV, 183, note 9). By contrast the man praying the Qumran psalms confessed that only God's spirit is able to bring a man to obey

tage point of his faith in the crucified One, he is describing the essence of his pre-Christian existence. This is the Adamite man under the Law, seen with the eye of faith. The model for the first part (Rom 7.7-13), written in the past tense, is Adam's fall. Sin, which at that time spoke from a serpent but now speaks from us, uses the commandment to voice its opposition to God and to force us into rebellion against God, that is, into death. The model for the second part (Rom 7.14-25), written in the present tense, is what the Pharisees did to Jesus: they wanted to do good and sanctify God's Law, but in guilty ignorance they did the opposite. The "I" in Rom 7 has become aware of the existence and at the same time the inescapability of this rebellion.[7] The total dilemma of the pre-Christian man is not only, as had been demonstrated for the Jew (Rom 2.20ff.; 9.31; 10.2f.), that he is caught in the schism between assenting and not performing, between longing for the righteousness of the Law and actually striving for self-righteousness; but he is also "fallen" in this dilemma and cannot escape it. He is "flesh." He wants to do good, but he cannot do it. Not until this self-awareness occurs does the way of salvation by the Law, that blueprint of Judaism, become impossible and the pre-Christian situation hopeless.

Who is that "wretched man" who with this knowledge cries for deliverance from "this body of death?" He is labeled neither Jew nor Christian. How is he related to either of them? If we begin by clarifying this man's relationship to the Christian it will also result in clarifying his relationship to the Jew. This will clarify the connection

---

the law: "I, however, belong to wicked mankind, to the mass of blasphemous flesh. . . . Surely no man decides his own way . . . but God is responsible for the decision and from his hand comes the perfect life . . . without him nothing can be done" (1 QS 11, 9-12, cf. 1 QH 4). This confession is reminiscent of Rom 7 and 8 and Gal 5. However, there is no mention in the Qumran texts of a conflict between the flesh and the "I."

[7] What the Jews do "in ignorance" (Lk 23.24; Acts 3.17; Rom 10.3) is "not understandable" for the "I" of Rom 7 (Rom 7.15a).

between the entire pre-Christian existence under the Law just sketched above and the Christian existence.

3. *Existence Under the Law Abolished by Existence Under the Gospel*

How is the "I" of Rom 7 related to the "I" of faith?[8] Rom 7 does not describe a chronologically past era, with man dismally at the end of his rope, that has now been replaced by a bright present. But neither does it reflect the battle which begins for faith between flesh and spirit (Gal 5.16-26) as Luther thought it did. In spite of the present tense, the "I" of Rom 7.14-25 is like the "I" of Rom. 7.7-13, in both cases basically past tense for the "I" of faith, but a past tense which always lies under the "I," not behind him in point of time. Man does not realize that this past existence is the "old man," the sinner, until he sees it in the light of God's consoling declaration of righteousness and is himself put to work by that righteousness. It is a past tense which time and time again becomes partially present experience for every Christian when faith and the Spirit decline. This is the situation of the old "I," which the Law forces out into the open when that Law is understood as a cross-oriented faith understands it: in keeping with Jesus' own proclamation it is both radical command (Rom 7.7) and exclusively retributive order (Rom 7.10f.).

The reality described in Rom 7.7-25 is present for faith and especially for faith because wherever the gospel is present it is present only as annulment of the Law. This reality is annulled for faith to the same extent that the Law is annulled by the gospel and concurrently the old "I" is crucified with Christ (Rom 6.1-11) and conquered by the Spirit (Rom 8.1-11; Gal 5.16-26).

The Law is annulled by the gospel as an order of sal-

[8] W. G. Kümmel, *Das Subjekt des 7. Kapitels des Römerbriefes* (Altenberg, 1929). P. Althaus, *Paulus und Luther über den Menschen* (3d ed.; Gütersloh, 1958).

vation (Rom 10.5; Gal 3.12): independent of works of the Law the believer receives righteousness, the blessed existence before God (Rom 3.21ff.; Gal 5.4). This annulment, however, occurs only on the basis of the vicarious atonement of the cross (Rom 3.25f.; Gal 3.13), through which the order of Law is sanctified. Therefore it occurs only for faith (Rom 10.5), which has crucified the old man with Christ, and is bound in living obedience to God (Rom 6.11 f.). Such faith is the fulfilling of the Law (Rom 7.4-6; Gal 2.19f.; Rom 8.3f.). Thus in faith's connection to Christ *the demands of law are annulled too*, and together with them all the national, social and sexual orders of this world.[9] This bond of faith with Christ embodies the fulfilling of the Law's central demand, as it is summarized in the second table of the decalog or in the command to love thy neighbor (Rom 13.8-10; Gal 5.14). At the same time by virtue this obedience's concreteness and radical character, the Old Testament national and ceremonial laws fall by the wayside of themselves. However, this concrete obedience operating on the freedom which faith grants still gives serious attention to the orders of this old world, which exist by virtue of God's creation or were concretely laid down in history to preserve life in creation.[10] The bond of faith with the crucified Christ, which as such directly encompasses the first table, is the annulment of God's present order superimposed upon this world, and as such it is the material principle, the basic building material, for an ethic which fulfills the Old Testament law.

Christ was "born under the law, to redeem those who were under the law" (Gal 4.4f.), that is, everyone. How little Jesus' death and resurrection abolished the Law in

---

[9] Rom 7.1ff.; 1 Cor 12.13; Gal 2.19f.; 3.27; 6.14f.; Col 2.20ff.; 3.11.
[10] Rom 13.1-7; Cor 3.21ff.; 6.12-20; 7; Col 3.18-4.1; Eph 5.22-6.9; cf. L. Goppelt, *The Freedom to Pay the Imperial Tax, Studia Evangelica II*, part II, *TU* 87 (Berlin, 1964).

any chronological sense can be seen in this, that all, even the believers, will be subject to its final retribution in the last judgment according to their works (2 Cor 5.10), and can hope for a final rescue only through the living crucified One (Rom 5.9). The cross, therefore, both separates and unites existence under the Law and existence under the gospel until the end of time. Consequently faith in the crucified One means not only being freed from the Law but also simultaneously affirming the ties of the old man and the old world to the Law (Rom 3.31).

But is there any genuinely empirical reality to this existence exclusively under the Law, from which Paul develops the absolute hopelessness of pre-Christian existence and its abolition through Christ as the sole deliverer (Gal 2.21; 5.2)? Is not the Law even in the Old Testament always and everywhere united with the promise of grace? The statements of Paul presented up to now still need to be verified in relation to redemptive history. We shall seek to supply this by clarifying the relationship of Law and promise.

4. The Antithesis Between Law and Promise

Measured by the empirical self-awareness of the Jew, Paul's presentation of pre-Christian existence is an abstract and distorted picture. No Jew can admit that the Law's demand of obedience is so radical (Rom 2.28f.) that it allows no compensation for works omitted by works achieved, but rather makes the existence of a man who really deserves the name "Jew" impossible. No Jew bases his existence exclusively on the order of retribution (Rom 10.5), but rather he places his hope in grace which supplements the adequacy of his obedience and takes his final refuge in the promise made to the fathers.[11]

[11] *Billerbeck*, I, 117ff. *Moore*, I, 535-45. Jewish historians have been emphasizing this for a long time. Most recently in Schoeps (Chap. IX,

In contrast to this *Paul justifies his presentation by a deep-going radical interpretation of the history of salvation* in Rom 4 and Gal 3.6-29. Jesus Himself had already in His earthly ministry drawn a sharp distinction between the Law, on the one hand, and the total commandment and total gift of grace which were being manifested through Him on the other. Paul takes up this distinction and *shatters the synthesis between Law and promise* which was Judaism's constitutive principle, and which the Old Testament itself had partially fostered. Abraham, he says, was pronounced righteous solely on the basis of his faith in the redemptive promise (Rom 4.18), apart from circumcision and Law, just as righteousness now is reckoned exclusively to faith in the redemptive fulfillment (Rom 4.24). The promise did not, as Judaism claimed in principle, "come through the law," but "through the righteousness of faith" (Rom 4.13), by grace (Rom 4.16). In Judaism, as time went on, the Law progressively incorporated the promise into itself. For Paul, however, the promise embraced the Law, but even then only as an expression of the certain abolition of the Law, and not as a supplement to the Law whereby prevenient grace would make existence under the Law possible. Grace is related exclusively to promise; it is achieved not by works, but only by faith. All of God's redemptive grace has its goal in the promise and its fulfillment; it was not intended to let the nation come to rest under the Law as was the case with Judaism, but rather to keep it in unrest until fulfill-

---

note 6), p. 218: "Because Paul had lost all understanding of the character of the Hebrew *berith* as a partnership involving mutual obligations, he failed to grasp the inner meaning of the Mosaic law, namely, that it is an instrument by which the covenant is realized. Hence the Pauline theology of law and justification begins with the fateful misunderstanding in consequence of which he tears asunder covenant and law, and then represents Christ as the end of the law." And again, pp. 261f.: "It must ever remain thought-provoking that the Christian church has received a completely distorted view of the Jewish law at the hands of a Diaspora Jew who had become alienated from the faith-ideas of the fathers." (Cf. Chap. IV, note 11.)

ment should come. Under the Law there is only retribution according to works (Gal 3.12; Rom 2.25ff.) and therefore in actuality only wrath (Rom 4.14f.). The goodness of God, which nevertheless made historical life under the Law possible (Gen 9), Paul does not call grace, but "patience," not forgiveness, but "forbearance" (Rom 3.25f.). This patience of God is terminated wherever through the gospel the righteousness of God is revealed (Rom 3.25). *The full gravity and despair of existence under the Law, therefore, does not dawn upon a man until he is under the gospel.*

We are now in a position to see the *difference between the two characterizations of pre-Christian existence in Romans and in Galatians.* According to Rom 7 the rule of the Law over man is deadly, and according to Gal 3 it is like that of the guardian over the heir while he is a child (Gal 3.23ff.; 4.1-5). Gal 3 refers to the historical pre-Christian condition in which the forbearance rules along with the Law. Existence under the covenant of the Law of Sinai is slavery (Gal 4.3ff., 25), but it is not the misery of being in "this body of death" (Rom 7.24). Rom 7, however, refers to the pre-Christian existence of him who already has been placed under the gospel, and therefore under the cross. On the cross the sentence on mankind pronounced by the radically understood Law was carried out for us (Gal 2.19; Rom 7.4; Gal 3.13). Consequently no one but the believer knows the radical and exclusive severity of pre-Christian existence under the Law. Not until he encounters the cross does he abandon what formerly was his righteousness (Phil 3.6f.).

What then is the meaning of the promise? The promise and all its exclusive redemptive grace are not intended to enable man to persist under the Law, but to direct him beyond it. The Law in its essential elements actually applies also to the Gentiles; the promise expressly includes the

Gentiles (Gal 3.8; Rom 4.16f.), but in contrast to Israel it was not addressed to them (cf. Eph 2.11f.). This constituted Israel's special prominence above the rest of humanity, which no analogous event could equal. However, it is only hinted at (Rom 3.2) in Rom 1-8, not spelled out. Here Paul is also taking this aspect of pre-Christian existence and viewing it in relation to faith in Christ. Perhaps Paul means to indicate that the patient waiting of God (Rom 3.25f.; Gal 4.3ff.) encompassed everyone in view of the fulfillment of the promise. But only this is really decisive, that in accord with the promise all are now called to faith in the fulfillment. Only that faith is saving faith which sees itself as the fulfillment of Abraham's faith (Rom 4.23-25); only that flock is the redeemed community which knows that it is the seed of Abraham (Gal 3.29), because *the Christ event is the fulfillment of "all the promises of God"* (2 Cor 1.20).

The letter to the Romans thus paints the *picture of a pre-Christian existence* that to the end of this world remains the significant place where existence under the gospel begins. This pre-Christian existence stands under the radically understood Law. The promise which also pertains to that existence finally has only one purpose, to call to faith in the gospel and thereby leave both that existence and the Law behind. This picture of pre-Christian existence is not an ethical-anthropological analysis of Judaism's pre-Christian history, but it kerygmatically describes where the believer comes from by interpreting Old Testament redemptive history in the light of the cross. Accordingly, this *pre-Christian existence can be labeled Judaism only insofar as it is actually represented by empirical Judaism.* Paul predicates to the Jews only their boasting about the Law without any corresponding fulfillment, and their pursuit of righteousness by the Law, which means striving for one's own righteousness. He does not predicate to them the

146

shattering experience of wanting and not being able, nor the patient waiting for the promise which looks only to God's grace. The permanent primeval ground and source of Christian existence is not empirical Judaism. But its ground and source, i.e., *genuine pre-Christian existence, is an existence* separated from empirical Judaism and *subsumed under an Old Testament that is itself interpreted in the light of the crucified and living Lord* (2 Cor 3.12-18; Gal 2.21; 5.2).

Rom 1-8 therefore is not an apologetic confrontation between the Christian message and Judaism. It is rather *Paul's conclusive statement of his gospel*, the message of the Christ event as the annulling fulfillment of the Old Covenant (cf. 2 Cor 3.14) and also the message of Christian existence as the annulment of the pre-Christian seen in this light. It is the Pauline gospel stated for the church that transcends both Jews and Gentiles as the redeemed community of the end-time (Rom 15.8-12; Gal 3.26-29; Col 3.10f.; Eph 2.11-22).

In this fashion Paul's gospel becomes the message of justification. Justification is not a polemic doctrine propounded by Paul to counter the Judaizers. Instead it is an expression of the core of the gospel which depicts that gospel as the goal of Old Testament redemptive history and the annulment of Judaism. "The cross" is the revelation of the righteousness of God since in the cross God has executed the sentence called for by the order of Law and has fulfilled the promise (Gal 3.13f.). Good Friday is the eschatological day of atonement; "God has publicly put Christ forward (on the cross) as an expiation by his (own) blood" (Rom 3.25). God has demonstrated that He is righteous, viz., that He is the one who acts in accordance with His covenant. Consequently the *gospel of Jesus Christ*, of His incarnation and His exaltation as expressed in the primitive church's confession cited in Rom 1.3f., is properly *interpreted as the gospel* of the revelation of the righteousness of God (Rom 1.16f.).

The gospel in Rom 1-8 does not have two different focuses, Rom 3 and Rom 6, but only one, the revelation of the righteousness of God. The righteousness of God, which came forth in the cross, declares the believer righteous gratuitously, i.e., it assigns him a place where he can, independent of his performance, survive before God (Rom 3.26), and simultaneously as a real power it makes him a "servant of righteousness" (Rom 6.18). Faith means faith in that God who raised from the dead our Lord Jesus, who "calls into existence the things that do not exist," who "reckons" a sinner righteous and gives life to the dead (Rom 4.6ff.,17,24f.). At the same time faith means "considering yourselves dead to sin and alive to God in Christ Jesus" (Rom 6.11). When Paul proclaims "dying with Christ" in order to "live with him" and the Christian life as "life in Christ," he is not erecting a second focus for his theology, a "Christ-mysticism" alongside of the "Christ for us" and justification of Rom 3. Instead the "with Christ" and "in Christ" of Rom 6 are consequences of the "Christ for us," since the righteousness of God, which came forth in the cross, is both gift and power. Already in the days of His earthly career Jesus Himself was "for" sinners in such a way that they were simultaneously called into discipleship "with" Him.

Righteousness of God is "the core theological concept of the Old Testament."[12] This concept corresponds most closely to the biblical manner of God's revelation. God does not encounter Israel as fate nor as a speaking oracle, but He encounters them as the one who through His word establishes a relationship between them and Himself, the one who makes a marriage with Israel. As a result the "highest value of life" for the Old Testament man is to be righteous,

12 v. Rad. (Chap. II, note 1), I, 370-83.

i.e., to satisfy this relationship with God. Pharisaic Judaism did not appropriate what the Old Testament said about God's righteousness,[13] but always reckoned only with individual acts of right or wrong. By contrast the psalms of Qumran speak impressively of being justified by the righteousness of God, for they knew that man's relationship with God is totally destroyed and has to be totally reconstituted.[14] Jesus' manner of speaking about repentance and forgiveness sounds at first like that of the Palestinian synagogue, but with these words He meant and actually provided a new relationship with God. In giving expression to this new relationship Paul's verb "*dikaioun*" ("to make righteous," in old English, "to right-wise," now translated in most English versions as "to justify") hits the nail right on the head. As a matter of fact Paul is led to this concept precisely because he sees the gospel from the perspective of Law and promise.

In the epistle to the Hebrews, which carries out an analogous exposition of the gospel, empirical Judaism no longer appears at all. In Romans, however, it appears first of all as an example of humanity in slavery to the law. In the realm of the Law Judaism has no advantage over the Gentiles, as will finally be seen at the last judgment (Rom 2.9f.), except the relative advantage of greater responsibility. But Paul cannot conclude his exposition of the gospel in this hour without raising the further question, "What then is the advantage of the Jew or the value of circumcision?" And he must answer, "Much in every way. They were entrusted with the oracles of God" (Rom 3.1f.). *God*

[13] *Billerbeck*, I, 250ff.; III, 163. Moore, I, 386-600.
[14] 1 QS 10,8-11,22, and 1 QH (1,21ff.; 7,28; 13,16f.). 1 QS 11,12 says: "But when I falter, then God's demonstrations of grace are my eternal deliverance; if my sinful flesh causes me to fall, my justification by God's righteousness will stand forever." See S. Schulz, "Zur Rechtfertigung aus Gnaden in Qumran und bei Paulus," ZThK, LVI (1959), 155-85.

had spoken to them, and what he said was in the first instance *a word of promise*. Judaism for Paul is therefore actually not, as it would appear from Gal 4.21-31, the existence exclusively under the covenant of Law given at Sinai. The concepts "Jew" and "circumcision" for him also have an aspect of promise about them. "Circumcision" is not only the obligation to keep the Law (Gal 5.3; Rom 2.25-29) that remains unachieved until the "circumcision without hands" (Col 2.11; Eph 2.11; Phil 3.2f.) takes place, but it is also the "seal" of having received the promise of salvation (Rom 4.11; 15.8). As the nation blessed with God's preliminary revelation of salvation, Israel in its Old Testament history is a type of the redeemed community of the end-time (1 Cor 10.1-13). Consequently it was the first to receive the announcement that the promise had been fulfilled (Rom 1.16; 15.8). But the special position granted Israel by the promise did not come to an end either with this priority proclamation of the gospel or with Israel's rejection of it. This is indicated by Rom 3.3 and the latter is treated extensively in Rom 9-11.

Chapter XII

Paul Interprets the Break: Part-Christian Israel and the Gospel (Romans 9–11)

1. The Problem of Romans 9–11

The existing interpretations of Rom 9-11[1] go their separate ways even in their understanding of what the problem is and not only in their attempts to solve it. Paul begins with an almost frantic assertion of his personal pain over Israel's fall. This itself may have given rise to the two most widely held misunderstandings: 1. Paul appears to be asking in terms of the theodicy question, How could God in His saving fulfillment have passed by His own people, which He Himself elected to salvation? Where is there any meaning in this fate of Israel? Older exegesis tended to give three answers to this question, but was able to muster only one of the three chapters for each of the answers. All three answers can be presented in the exposition of Rom 11.25f. The first says that all those who are predestined will be saved; Rom 9 supports it. The second, the indeterministic answer, says that all who are ready to believe will be saved; Rom 10 backs it up. The third, the answer from redemptive history, says that after a temporary hardening the whole people will be saved; its grounds are Rom 11. More recent

[1] For the history of the exegesis see E. Weber, *Das Problem der Heilsgeschichte nach Römer 9-11* (Leipzig, 1911). More recent literature, exclusive of the commentaries, on Romans: K. Barth, *Church Dogmatics*, II/2 (Edinburgh, 1957), 195-305. G. Schrenk, *Die Weissagung über Israel im Neuen Testament* (Zurich, 1951). K. L. Schmidt; *Die Judenfrage im Lichte der Kapitel 9-11 des Römerbriefes.* (2d ed.; 1947). W. Vischer, "Das Geheimnis Israels," *Judaica*, VI (1950), 81-132. J. Munck, *Christus und Israel. Eine Auslegung von Römer 9-11* (Copenhagen, 1956). J. Munck, *Paul* (Richmond, Virginia, 1959), pp. 42-49. L. Goppelt, "Israel and the Church, Today's View and Paul's View," *Lutheran World*, X, No. 4 (1963), 352-72.

exegesis acknowledges the fallacy of subordinating the answers given by two chapters to that of a third. It sees Paul developing a number of perspectives, which successively replace each other. Such interpretations all remain unsatisfactory because they wrongly take the theodicy to be the real question.

2. This applies all the more to the *psychological-apologetic phrasing of the question*: How could the people best prepared for faith refuse to believe? or, Is Israel not a case where the missionary power of the word failed?

In actual fact the *problem in Rom 9-11 grows directly out of the prophetic interpretation of the historical situation* that characterizes the entire composition of the epistle (see p. 134) *and out of* the train of thought pursued in *the first eight chapters.* Rom 8 closes with the great hymn of the certainty of salvation. Through Israel's fate, however, that certainty seems to waver. Paul's pain over Israel's unbelief arises not only from his natural tie with his people, which the apostle never denied (2 Cor 11.22; Phil 3.5), but all the more from his knowledge about this people's original destiny: "They are Israelites" (Rom 9.4). God had promised sonship to this people, imparted His glory and His gracious presence to them, placed them in covenant relationship with Himself, and granted them His Law, a worship corresponding to His will, and also the promises (Rom 9.4). It is first of all to this people that the patriarchs belong, with whom the history of God's salvation and promise began, and from this people God, confirming all this, brought forth Jesus, the fulfillment (Rom 9.5). When Paul thinks of this, a question arises in him which he does not dare to express, but which he represses in a prayer of praise to God, and then answers in Rom 9.6 (cf. Rom 11.29): "It is not as though the word of God had failed."

Has God's calling and promising word failed? Has He been untrue to Himself? Has He proved to be "un-right-

152

eous?" *This is the question of Rom 9-11;* all of the gifts of salvation enumerated in Rom 9.4 are based on the word of promise. But at the same time this very question is the life-and-death question of faith, to which Rom 1-8 leads. Does not our share in the sonship, the glory, and God's covenant ultimately rest solely and alone on God's promise? Does not our certainty of salvation, according to Rom 8.29f., rest only on this, that He who has called us will also lead us to the goal? *The question of Israel's salvation is synonymous with the ultimate question of Christian theology and Christian faith.* Rom 9-11 is not an appendix to the letter to the Romans. It actually is the keystone which closes the arch of Paul's theology and holds it all together.

Thus Rom 9-11 is not an attempt to understand a psychological riddle or the philosophy of history. What we have here is *a prayerful wrestling with God Himself,* with the principle of His rule in redemptive history. Therefore the chapters do not describe a step-by-step penetration into God's plans, but rather a step-by-step *self-disclosure by God* for faith. It is not an intelligible process of history which becomes evident, but here it is the righteousness of God (in the sense in which Paul has earlier developed it) which becomes ever brighter and more certain to the faith that submits to it. And for this reason Rom 11 does not close with a summary of the knowledge that has been gained, but rather with adoration and praise of the unsearchable "depth of the riches and wisdom and knowledge of God."

2. *The First Answer*

In Rom 9.6-29 the first answer is given: *God's word of promise from the very beginning meant only those elected by God's free grace.* Even in the history of the patriarchs it is clear that not the descendants according to the flesh, but rather only those designated by God's free grace—equally independent of any human works—are heirs of the promise

(Rom 9.6-13; cf. Gal 4.22f.). Is not this action of God arbitrary; is He not "unjust"? No! God still remains true to Himself in this; He always saves on the basis of His free mercy, never on the basis of human qualifications. Even by hardening hearts at the same time God proves that His saving action is free grace (Rom 9.14-18).

Does not this destroy all of man's responsibility? "Why does he still find fault?" (Rom 9.19.) Whoever asks this forgets that he is speaking with God and not with a man. God is not our equal partner, but rather He through whom everything is, and who yet holds us responsible to Him. However, when Paul describes us as clay in the potter's hand, he does not intend to silence us in speechless obeisance under the speculative notion of double predestination. We do not stand as observers before an eternal decision of God, but we are here face to face with God's election in redemptive history that actually precipitates in God's historically calling those whom He elected.[2] *In the face of God's action in wrath and grace we who are granted grace are called to faith and praise.* In allowing unbelieving Israel to remain God is expressing the wrath which gives up sin to sin, and also expressing the power by which He can exclude anyone from the kingdom. In the face of such action by God you finally realize what grace is (Rom 9.19-23).

Has God's word failed? A series of scriptural quotations, Rom 9.24-29, shows that in calling His church from Jews and Gentiles *God has fulfilled His word of promise* in the way it was intended from the beginning. Excluding

[2] "To call" for Paul means as a rule "to bring to faith." In only one place, Rom 11.28, where it is predicated of Israel, does it mean merely calling out to someone, but even here this calling will someday bring Israel to faith. The "called," however, are for Paul also the ones "predestined" and the "elect" (Rom 8.29f.). Paul knows nothing about an election which does not become historically manifest in being called in precisely this sense.

every claim of flesh or of works (Rom 9.12; 11.6), God has always called into His redeemed community only those whom He had elected according to His free grace. Those called from Israel constitute the promised "*remnant*" (Rom 9.27). It is in this connection, and not before this, that we have the first instance of primitive Christian theology appropriating the Old Testament idea of the "remnant."

3. *The Second Answer*

God's faithfulness would therefore still be unimpaired even if He had simply bypassed the mass of Israel with His revelation of salvation. Actually He acted in a completely different fashion. The second answer, Rom 9.30-10.21, says that *God has called all of Israel to salvation far above and beyond His word of promise, but Israel has refused it to its own guilt.*

The concrete historical events that led to *the present situation* in redemptive history were on the surface highly offensive (Rom 9.30; 10.3). Just as the tax collectors and prostitutes had entered God's kingdom in the days of Jesus' earthly ministry, so the *Gentile nations*, who had never shown an interest in being righteous before God, were now adjudged righteous on the basis of their faith. But *Israel*, which constantly strove to be righteous,[3] was never adjudged to be so. Actually, however, this zeal of Israel was only a deceit, the most infamous form of sin. Israel pursued the "law of righteousness," the Law that pronounced righteous whoever fulfilled it (Rom 10.5). But Israel had not "succeeded in fulfilling that law," had not united itself with it. Why not? Not only because it could not fulfill the Law in its entire breadth and depth (Rom 2.17-24), but also because its striving itself was already wrong. Israel's striving for righteousness by the Law was, as Rom 7 shows, inevi-

[3] For Paul, as it was for Jesus, Judaism is represented by the Pharisaic mentality. Secularized or indifferent Jews in this connection are irrelevant.

tably a striving for "their own righteousness." They were really seeking what the brother of the prodigal son was seeking, not unification with the Law but rather their own worthiness. One's "own righteousness" is the recognition to which man lays claim by virtue of his fulfilling the Law.

God sets one last stumbling block in the way of this striving for one's own righteousness over which Israel finally trips (Rom 9.33), namely, the crucified Christ. Just how this happens is shown by the Pharisees' anger at Jesus' acceptance of "sinners," and the Jews' offense at the crucified Christ who brought all self-pride to nought (1 Cor 1.23; Gal 5.11; 6.12ff.).

In order to condemn this inevitable and ultimate slavery to sin and to free them from it, God replaced the mediatory role of the Law with that of Christ, not in chronological sequence, but "for every one who has faith" (Rom 10.4-13). Nevertheless in their pursuit of self-righteousness they remain "ignorant of the righteousness that comes from God" (Rom 10.2f.). This ignorance is not a tragic mistake, but rather a guilty blindness that also characterizes the religious efforts of the Gentiles (Eph 4.18). Thus Israel rejects in guilty disobedience the message of the liberating righteousness of faith that was proclaimed to them just as it was to the Gentiles (Rom 10.14-18).

Behind the God of Rom 9, who proves that His merciful faithfulness is free grace to His chosen ones by the very hardening of the hearts of others, the God in Rom 10 reveals himself to faith as the one who in immeasurable mercy holds out His hands to a people that will not accept fellowship with Him but prefer to assert themselves before Him with the help of the Law, and thus refuse His grace. In prayerful submission to God's free grace, Rom 9 takes Israel's unbelief to be God's judgment which hardens hearts, i.e., locks faith out; independently from this Rom 10 acknowledges it as the standing guilt of Israel's disobedience, rooted in the profound wickedness of humanity.

156

This double realization, Rom 9 and 10, presenting in itself an insoluble antinomy, is as far as almost all the rest of the New Testament goes in the face of Israel's unbelief.[4] But Paul is led even deeper into God's redemptive will.

4. *The Problem of Paul's Question in Romans 11.1*

Surprisingly enough Paul starts to question anew in Rom 11.1 whether "God has rejected his people." Does this mean that he has abandoned what he said in Rom 9.6ff.? Is it true after all that Israel includes more than just those elected (Rom 9.6b)? Stauffer gives this explanation: In Rom 11 "the Spirit of Jesus triumphed over the spirit of anti-Semitism and the polemics of the oppressed (1 Thess 2,14ff.), and the realism of his theology of history displaced his first attempts at allegory (Gal 3.16) and spiritualization (Rom 9.8). Israel is by race the children of Abraham and the people of the promise (Rom 3.2f.; 4.1; 9.4f.). But these promises are irrevocable (Rom 3.3f.; 11.29)."[5]

Stauffer's statement throws the whole question of interpreting Rom 1-11 into bold relief, but his acceptance of various Pauline "points of view" leads him to erroneous answers. Gal 3 and Rom 9 simply cannot be dismissed as "first attempts," for in spite of the questionable character of some of Paul's own exegesis in these two sections, both are developed straight out of the doctrine of justification. In Gal 3 and Rom 4 the doctrine of justification by faith decrees that only those in Christ are Abraham's seed, and in Rom 9 that only those from Israel who have entered the church are the true Israel (Rom 9.6). But nevertheless it is that very faith which has abandoned all boasting of flesh and works, as these anti-Judaizing assertions show, and has

[4] Mk 4.11 par.; Mt 23.37 par. Lk; Acts 28.25-28; Jn 12.37-40. J. Gnilka, *Die Verstockung Israels. Jes. 6, 9-11 in der Theologie der Synoptiker* (Munich, 1961).

[5] *New Testament Theology* (New York, 1955), p. 192.

157

taken recourse to God's word of election alone, which may and must raise this question. In opposition to all of the church's self-conceit and for the sake of its own certainty of salvation it must ask: Has God rejected that people which as a whole had received all the things mentioned in Rom 9.4f.? In Rom 11 Paul is not proposing another theory to replace all that he has said before. Instead *he presents the other side of an antinomy that is valid only when seen together with what has been said before.* Our subsequent analysis will seek to substantiate this.

5. *The Third Answer*

Rom 11.2-10 shows how little Paul has abandoned what he said before, for here he is in essence simply repeating the first answer in Rom 9. God has not rejected His people, for His people are there in the saved remnant. Those who have fallen are not referred to as God's people here either. But a different tone runs through this repetition of the first answer. There the word was: only a remnant. Here it is: *already a remnant!*

Paul begins with a reference to himself (Rom 11.1). More than any other member of his people Paul had fallen prey to that zeal for the Law which was blind to Christ. The grace that saved him can save everyone. But with his lamentation about Israel (Rom 9.1f.; 10.1) he seems to stand before God as lonesome as Elijah on Horeb (Rom 11.2-6; cf. 1 Kings 19.9ff.). Such a comparison illuminates the very depths of the situation in Rom 9-11. This is the posture in which Paul inquires and this is the posture in which he receives God's illuminating and comforting counsel. Together with Paul a remnant has already been saved. Israel in that day stands in God's grace no less than in the days of Elijah.

So Paul risks the ultimate question: *"Have they stumbled so as to fall [forever]?"* (Rom 11.11.) Is their falling

158

an end in itself? Is it final? At first faith might fear that Israel's hardened antagonism against Christ and His church is but the final eternal wrath of God in action. This is the sense in which 1 Thess 2.15f. must be seen, for despite its hints of ancient anti-Semitism, it is a parallel to Rom 9.22. Faith takes seriously the fact that Israel was actually called in history and views this fact as the realization of God's foreknowledge and election (Rom 8.29). But it is precisely this factor of God's "foreknowledge" in Rom 11.2 which now imposes this question upon him.

To this questioning faith the following unfolds: *Israel's falling is not an end in itself*. Because of it the reconciliation was accomplished in the cross (Rom 11.15a), and especially because of it the message was forced out to the nations. But the Gentiles' appropriating salvation ought to make Israel "jealous." Their fleshly jealousy in Acts 13.45 and Rom 10.19 should be transmuted into a holy jealousy. If Israel's falling has already meant so much salvation for the nations of the world, then Israel's own redemption can mean nothing less than the dawn of the culmination of all salvation (Rom 11.12-15).

In moving to the next step of clarifying Israel's future Paul proceeds in a strictly kerygmatic pattern. The *salvation of Israel is possible* (Rom 11.16-24). The Gentile Christians (they are meant in these verses with the term Gentiles) have no reason to scorn fallen Israel in Pharisaic self-satisfaction instead of longing for its conversion. Even though only the elect are the seed of the promise and by now a part of the redeemed community (Rom 9.8ff.), yet all the natural children of Abraham (at least in keeping with 1 Cor 7.14) are sanctified (Rom 11.16), ordained to be God's possession. Israel is like a choice olive tree, those rejecting Christ like withered branches, the Gentile Christians like newly grafted branches from a wild olive tree. This illustration seeks to express the continuity of God's saving

159

activity in history: God ties himself to men. Consequently salvation is to be found only in historical continuity by inheriting the promises given to the fathers: The Gentile Christians are what they are only because they have become "Abraham's seed." Consequently there is still hope for unbelieving Israel. The illustration certainly does not say that Israel's election was, so to speak, inherently intrinsic, so that the branches which had been cut off would obviously be restored. The illustration seeks precisely to prevent all security. The continuity rests solely upon God's faithfulness. Consequently the Christians' attitude toward unbelieving Israel is a touchstone for their own self-awareness. They do not stand in faith unless they confess that the grace which saved them can also save those most hopelessly lost, therefore, above all, the severed branches of the people of the old covenant. They are in faith only if it is their "heart's desire that they may be saved" (Rom 10.1), and if they are certain that this petition in spite of everything is not hopeless, but that "God is able to graft them in again" by bringing them to faith.

The possibility of conversion exists, but will it be realized? In order that the Christians may not harbor their own arbitrary thought about Israel's future, Paul reveals to them a "mystery," a portion of God's plan of salvation announced to him by revelation, which will come true in the last days: "A hardening has come upon part of Israel, until the full number of the Gentiles come in, and so all Israel will be saved." The "full number of the Gentiles" does not mean "all Gentiles, without exception," nor the Gentiles predestined to be saved, but rather that multitude of Gentiles comparable to the richness of the grace of God. "And so," that is, after the fulfillment of this prerequisite, after this hardening of part of Israel and the salvation of the Gentiles made possible by it, "all Israel will be saved." "All Israel," analogous to the full number of the Gentiles, does not mean the sum of all the members of the Jewish people, nor the host of the predestined in Israel, but Israel as a whole people.[6] When all Israel is saved, there may yet be indifferent, unbelieving Jews, but there will then no longer be a synagogue nor any Jews who reject Jesus on the basis of their own Law.

How this prediction is to be fulfilled is not spelled out, as in all genuine prophecy. Paul probably thinks of it as a miraculous event coming just before the impending Parousia of Christ (Rom 13.11f.) and following the conversion of the nations, perhaps even caused by this conversion; for according to Rom 11.15 Israel's conversion means the dawn of the final fulfillment.

6. *Testing the Prediction in Romans 11.25f.*

This prophecy is almost unique in the New Testament. Revelation, the book of the final history of the church, is conspicuously silent concerning the future of the Jewish nation in redemptive history.[7] This silence here, as in John's gospel, is not accidental, nor is it a rejection of Rom 11. It is caused rather by a difference in impetus between Paul's and John's writings. The disciples' question about restoring the kingdom to Israel (Acts 1.6f.) and the ancient call to Israel to repent (Acts 3.19-21) must be understood strictly in their historical situations. They are the results of the old biblical idea that the redemption of the world begins with the conversion of Israel. This was refuted by the actual course of mission work, but not the expectation of Israel's being saved after its fall. Eliminating this distinction robs Rom 11.25f. of its impact. In the whole New Testament only *Jesus' words* retained in the synoptic tradition in Mt 23.39 par. Lk have a disposition similar to Rom 11.25f.

[6] This way of speaking occurs already in 1 Kgs 12.1; 2 Chr 2.1.
[7] Neither Rev 7.1-8 nor Rev 11, in particular 11.13, nor Rev 20.1-10, in particular 20.9, say anything about it!

Perhaps the version in Matthew is a direct parallel. These prophetic words of Paul, in the face of Jewish rejection of his missionary proclamation of the crucified One, renew the promise which those words of Jesus express in the face of Israel's rejection of Jesus' earthly work.

This bold prediction had *an uneven reception in the subsequent history of the church.*[8] The church of the second century ignored Rom 11.25f. Not until the chiliasm of the third century, when the church was already beginning to outlaw it, do several hints appear about a redemptive turn in Israel's destiny before the end.[9] The great exegetes of the ancient church to a great extent lacked an internal appreciation of Paul's core theological concern to understand fully the sense of Rom 11.25f. Since Joachim von Flora and especially since Pietism, a conversion of Israel before the end has been taught in *chiliastic eschatology,*[10] but less in the sense of Rom 11.25f. than for the sake of a "realistic" fulfillment of the Old Testament prophecy. It is noteworthy that Luther rejected chiliasm, but retained the expectation of Rom 11.25f. Two examples may reflect the judgment of more recent Protestant theology on Rom 11.25f. Adolf von Harnack[11] was shocked by this expectation that the patriarchal promises would be someday fulfilled in a special way to the natural descendants of Abraham, thereby giving the Jewish people a special religious position. This, he said, was one of the "Jewish blinders" beyond which Paul, bound by his personal back-

[8] K. H. Schelkee, *Paulus Lehrer der Väter. Die altkirchliche Auslegung von Römer 1-11* (Düsseldorf, 1956), pp. 400ff.

[9] Victorin of Pettau, Commentary on Rev 20, *CSEL*, XLIX, 140; cf. Commodian, *Carm. apologetic.*, 927-98.

[10] P. Althaus, *Die letzten Dinge* (8th ed.; Gütersloh, 1961) pp. 299-304.

[11] *Lehrbuch der Dogmengeschichte*, I (5th ed.; Tübingen, 1931/32), 99f. This pejorative reference occurs only beginning with Harnack's 4th ed. It is already dimly reflected in the English ed., *History of Dogma* (Boston, 1900ff., republished New York, 1961), translated from Harnack's 3d ed. (I, 89ff.).

ground, never progressed and which impaired his effectiveness in the Gentile church of the second century considerably. A distinctly contrary view is the detailed systematic meditation of Karl Barth on Rom 9-11 in his comments on Rom 11.26:[12] "The 'mystery' does not in any sense consist in a change which we can one day expect in relation to Israel; in the reingrafting, according to the nature of Israel and in establishment of its election, of branches which are now severed. . . . The latter will indeed be the natural event already announced and prepared by the calling and conversion of the Gentiles, and in a twofold sense definitely to be expected along with it. The mystery, on the other hand, consists in the hiddenness of the meaning of the fact that this event has not yet taken place. This 'all Israel' (the community of those elected by God in and with Jesus Christ both from Jews and also from Gentiles) will be saved in the way which is now disclosed in the relationship of the Church and the Synagogue, that is, in such a way that the first will be last and the last first."

This central New Testament insight is, however, not the central thought of this passage. Barth's interpretation conflicts not only with the sense of the words "and so" and "Israel," but also with the actual intention of Rom 9-11. He understands election too much as predestination outside of history and too little as an event within redemptive history as one waits in fear and trembling for the actual saving call.

In the face of this frequent misunderstanding and disregard, the prophecy in Rom 11.25f. is to be "tested" according to the apostle's own directions (1 Cor 12.10; 14.29; 1 Thess 5.21). Paul himself gives an internal confirmation of his prophecy in Rom 11.26-32. He first points to one single prophecy in the scriptures (Rom 11.26f.). He does not want to derive his prophecy from the Old Testament

[12] Church Dogmatics, II/2, 299f.

one, but in the latter he finds it confirmed. The interpretation of the prophetic Old Testament and New Testament fulfillment stand for Paul in a mutual correspondence originating from the latter (2 Cor 3.16), whereby in substance this statement applies: For faith the fulfillment of all promises is present, though hidden, in Jesus Christ (2 Cor 1.20). Paul does not deduce from the thesis of the *irrevocability of God's call* (Rom 9.6), repeated in the concluding verses, Rom 11.28f., a postulate for the final conversion of Israel; this was already clear in Rom 11.1. But surely what has been revealed concerning Israel's future is a confirmation of the faithfulness of God's calling word, which is the whole point in these three chapters, surpassing and overwhelming all imagination. It is in its own right a prophecy that corresponds to the *analogia fidei* (analogy of faith). As the prophecy thus proves true on the basis of God's action in redemptive history, so also according to the powerful closing statements in Rom 11.30-32 on *the basis of God's saving action through Christ:* "God has consigned all men to disobedience, that he may have mercy upon all" (Rom 11.32). God's wrath stands in the service of his love!

This is surely no universal truth, but rather the ultimate certainty granted to faith through the cross (Rom 5.5-8). It is at this point that this certainty and the revelation concerning Israel's destiny mutually confirm each other. Accordingly verse 32 does not express the idea of the restitution of all, a notion nourished largely by unbiblical cyclical thought. Philologically, after all, the Greek word translated "all," means the totality, not every individual. Actually here the principle of redemption through Christ is being proclaimed, which characterizes the redeeming work of the end-time beginning with the earthly ministry of Jesus and reaching to the final homecoming of Israel. As Jesus called the righteous to come over to the sinners, so Israel is called to come over to the Gentiles. Redemptive

164

history does not move toward fulfillment in a straight line according to the rule, "the Jew first, then the Gentiles," but rather in a zig-zag brought about by the cross, which annihilates all of man's boasting.

Can we accept this internal confirmation which Paul gives to his prophecy? The prophecy was not fulfilled in the way Paul imagined it. The fullness of the Gentiles, which was to precede the conversion of Israel, failed to appear and so did the imminent Parousia that was to follow it. The writings of John and Luke, one generation later, try to do justice to the new situation. Does not Rom 11.25f. also fall along with the expectation of an imminent Parousia? We cannot regard this prophecy, as is often done today, as an almost self-evident postulate derived from the prophecy and redemptive history of the Old Testament and from general statements about God's love and faithfulness. Even less, however, can we see in it an expression of Jewish prejudice, as Harnack does. We can only "test," as Paul does, whether it stems from the Spirit of the crucified—and agree with his internal confirmation. The grace of God, which Paul himself encountered in the cross (Rom 11.1), led him already in Rom 5.18f. to risk the statement, independent of the question of Israel, that Christ meant salvation inclusively for all, even as Adam meant condemnation for all. Only the faithfulness of God, which overcomes all human unfaithfulness, gives him and his congregations certainty of salvation (1 Cor 1.5-9; Phil 2.12f.), in the face of all failures. This love and this faithfulness of God, which are revealed in the cross, give us also the right to hope that the work of salvation which came to Israel as a people (Rom 9.4f.; 11.16), in spite of Israel's unfaithfulness (Rom 10) and contrary to all human claims (Rom 9), but in accord with redemptive prophecy which continually points to God's creatio ex nihilo (cf. Ezek 37), will be perfected as gloriously as is proclaimed by the revelation in

Rom 11.25f. Israel's unique self-assertion and continued existence in history is a confirmatory sign of this, but no more.

What significance does this continuing existence of Israel have for the church? Rom 1-8 fundamentally separates the Law and promise of the Old Testament from the historical existence of Judaism. The gospel has constitutive connection only with Old Testament Law and promise and not with historical Judaism. In keeping with Rom 11.17-24, *the existence of unbelieving Israel is a historical touchstone for the church, but not a prerequisite for its existence in redemptive history.* What is the church to see in the Israel that has rejected Christ? It is not the anti-Christianity of a post-Christian era. Its unbelief is not a falling away from Christ, but a rejection of Jesus based on misuse of the revelation of the Law and on blindness concerning Christ's subsequent annulment of the Law (Rom 9.30-10.4; 2 Cor 3.12-18). Thus this Judaism, too, is in its actions a prime example of pre-Christian humanity. But its "enmity" against God and His Christ is not simply that of the world, which is still loved by God in Jesus Christ (Rom 5.6ff.). *Unbelieving Israel is not just a portion of the world.* They are "enemies of God for your sake," *"beloved for the sake of their forefathers"* (Rom 11.28). Their enmity is negative service to the gospel. Their being loved for the sake of their forefathers, compared with everyone being loved in Christ, is an expression of the promise applying specially to them. Unbelieving Israel, therefore, is not that portion of the congregation of God still unbelieving, nor the opposite counterpart of the church, but rather the opposite counterpart of the ancient people of the covenant, the people which maintains against Christ (Rom 9.30-10.4; 2 Cor 3.12-18) the covenant with God abolished by Christ (Rom 9.4). History shows to what great extent the church's *position toward this unbelieving Israel became a test for its*

166

own *self-awareness*. The church that banned unbelieving Israel into the ghetto in order to gain from Israel's misfortune the proof of its own rights in theological history has misunderstood itself just as profoundly as the church that flattered itself with its propagation of tolerance toward the venerable religion of Judaism. Only the church that views unbelieving Israel in the light of Rom 9-11 will be divorced from all false security in its own salvation and all contempt toward those who have fallen; only such a church will become aware of the nature of its own existence by grace alone. From Rom 11 it will gain an ultimate certainty of salvation for itself and an ultimate confidence also for all the baptized who fall away. It will also be performing the service it owes to Israel, namely, unabridged witness to Christ.

Romans stands at the center of the primitive history of the church as the conclusive and most comprehensive directive on the question of Christianity and Judaism. His commission to be the apostle to the Gentile nations obligated Paul to administer the redemptive mystery revealed to him, namely, that the Gentiles in Christ should be fellow heirs of the promise through the gospel (Eph 3.6), that God in Christ had abolished the dividing wall of the Law separating Jews from Gentiles and both from God, and that God had reconciled both with Himself as a new creation in one body, the church (Eph 2.16). The prospect in Rom 11 of Israel's homecoming after the Gentiles have come in crowns Paul's stunning vision of God's redemptive economy which the Spirit of the crucified Lord had disclosed to him.

Chapter XIII

Paul's Conflict with Jewish Gnosticism: The Initial Conflict with Syncretism

The farther the church moved away from the realm of Judaism, the more it had to struggle to assert itself in Hellenistic territory.[1] Long before the conflict with nomistic Judaism reached the temperative conclusion already described, the church was drawing up its defenses against syncretistic undermining. Surprisingly enough, the most dangerous threat from syncretism came into the church first of all from Judaism. Consequently this phase of the church's history is part of our overall theme. Coming to terms with such events was the key issue of the early apostolic age, and can be traced in the first large congregation in Hellenistic territory of whose beginnings we have more accurate information, namely, Corinth. The Corinthian solution to this issue will show whether the reconstruction we have made up to now is correct or not. The historical construction of the Tübingen school, whose effects are still felt today, was that nomistic Judaism from Galatia was also at work in Corinth. In contrast to this, however, since the work of W. Lütgert investigators have realized more and more that the opposition to Paul's teaching in Corinth originated not from a nomistic, but a gnostic Judaism.[2]

[1] P. Wendland, Die hellenistisch-römische Kultur (2d and 3d eds.; Tübingen, 1912). M. P. Nilsson, History of Greek Religion (2d ed.; Oxford, 1949). W. W. Tarn, Hellenistic Civilisation (2d ed.; London, 1952). M. Rostovtzeff, Social and Economic History of the Hellenistic World. 3 vols. (Oxford, 1941); 2 vols. (new ed., 1957). C. K. Barrett, The New Testament Background (London, 1956). F. C. Grant, Hellenistic Religions (New York, 1953). Th. Klauser (ed.), Reallexikon für Antike und Christentum (Stuttgart, 1950ff.).

[2] W. Lütgert, Freiheitspredigt und Schwarmgeister in Korinth (Gütersloh, 1908). A. Schlatter, Die korinthische Theologie (Gütersloh,

168

1. Pneumatic Judaism in Corinth

a. The "False Apostles" of Second Corinthians

The opponents who taught against Paul in Corinth are immediately apparent in 2 Cor 10-13. Here our investigation must begin. As wandering evangelists the opponents had come into the congregations Paul had established. Paul disputed not the content of their proclamation, but their understanding of their office. They called themselves "apostles of Christ" (2 Cor 11.13; cf. 10.7) and "servants of righteousness" (2 Cor 11.15), and challenged Paul's apostleship. This challenge to Paul was not, as had been the case in Galatia, simply to support their proclamation of the gospel, but first and last to establish the authority of their office.

They sought to establish their identity in two different respects. First they called attention to their historical connection with the source of the gospel. They were "Hebrews," not Diaspora Jews estranged from the Holy Land, "Israelites," members of the people of salvation, "descendants of Abraham" and at the same time "servants of Christ" (2 Cor 11.22). Most likely they boasted of close ties with Jesus' earthly ministry or at least to the immediate eyewitnesses of His ministry, and accordingly they submitted letters of recommendation from the Jerusalem congregation (2 Cor 3.1; 5.16). They apparently wanted to legitimize their activity and teaching by means of a documented commission and succession, which would prove that the tradition they represented was genuine; this was a Jewish principle.[3] In this manner these evangelists, perhaps comparable

---

1914). A. Schlatter, Paulus, der Bote Jesu (3d ed.; Stuttgart, 1962). D. Georgi, Die Gegner des Paulus im 2. Korintherbrief (Neukirchen, 1963) (contains a survey of the recent discussion, which has not produced anything that moves beyond Schlatter). Cf. the various commentaries and New Testament introductions on the Corinthian epistles.

[3] Billerbeck, II, 647-61. Moore, I, 109, 255f.

to the emissaries which Judaism sent from Jerusalem, sought to be authorized messengers, apostles.

Although this form of authorization through Jewish canons of legitimation is reminiscent of the Galatian Judaizers, it was thoroughly overlaid with a *pneumatic authorization* that was foreign to nomistic Judaism. The details are but dimly reflected in Paul's polemic. Perhaps the opponents boasted of visions which gave them the aura of ambassadors of the other world (2 Cor 3.7; 12.1-10). They demonstrated their pneumatic authorization by mighty works (2 Cor 12.12). They were superior to Paul in fluency of speech, that is, probably not with reference to rhetorical ability (2 Cor 11.6), but rather to the art of speaking freely and spontaneously, which was a sign of the pneumatic man in Hellenism. Their thoughts were the high-flown cogitations of autocratic reason (2 Cor 10.4f.).

Thus according to them *the Pneuma* without exception turned out to be a supernatural, other-worldly power. According to Paul the Pneuma was the power which shattered historical existence in order to achieve service "in weakness" (2 Cor 12.10). The opponents sneered at this "weakness," which waited in self-denying service for the power of the resurrected Lord (2 Cor 3.4-18; 4.7ff.). They labeled this peculiarly halting behavior "in weakness" as "fleshly," because they looked only on the surface (2 Cor 10.2). Paul could forego the apostle's right for support, but for them the claim to an expense account clearly expressed their understanding of their office. But a Pneuma that completed rather than replaced the "sufficiency of ourselves" (2 Cor 3.5) could not be the Pneuma of the crucified Christ. The "boasting"[4] characteristic of Paul's opponents transformed the Pneuma and all his gifts into a means for human self-assertion. It came to a head in their challenge

[4] 2 Cor 10.8,13, 15ff.; 11.10,12,16f., 18,30; 12.1,9,11; cf. Bultmann, καυχάομαι *TWNT*, III, 648ff.

to Paul's apostleship, which showed more clearly than any subtle formal doctrinal difference that they were promoting "another Jesus, a different spirit, a different gospel" (2 Cor 11.4). Since their basic concepts, which sounded the same as Paul's, had a different content, everything in their message was different from Paul's proclamation (2 Cor 11.13ff.).

The content of this "different gospel" (2 Cor 11.4) therefore was not at all a nomistic Judaizing restrained until these apostles established the authority of their own apostolic office. Nor was it simply the errors which Paul combatted in Second Corinthians, although it certainly was a source of them.[5]

b. *The Pneumatics in First Corinthians*

The errors First Corinthians faces were not regressions into heathenism, as could happen any time in a newly founded congregation on Greek soil. These errors were rather the consistent consequences of a basic position which passed for pneumatic freedom in the congregation.[6] Behind this attitude stood a peculiar mixture of Jewish and Hellenistic conceptions. Not only Paul, but even the Corinthian Christians viewed the problems in connection with Jewish presuppositions. The reason for this is not only because some of the problems arose from the conservative Jewish Christians in the congregation, but also because fundamentally the problems were of Jewish origin. This applies to the questions of meat offered to idols, head coverings for women, and the Christian use of Gentile courts of law, as well as to the questions of sexual mores and even the Resur-

[5] Schlatter noted that not everything which happened in Corinth originated with them, but it happened while they were exerting the strongest influence.

[6] 1 Cor 1.11f.; 3.1-4; 4.8; 5.1f.,6; 6.12f.; 7.40; 8.1ff.; 9.1; 13.4; 14.1; 15.12.

rection.[7] In the Corinthian congregation the decisions on all these questions had come from the "wisdom" of the "wise," who are criticized in the initial chapters (1-4) of the letter. This "wisdom" was not wisdom in the Greek sense, knowledge of the world, but rather knowledge of God's will; and yet neither was it wisdom in the Old Testament Jewish sense, but in a paradoxical revision of the Old Testament concept it was absolute knowledge (1 Cor 1.20; 8.1). Their principal judgment, expressed in the formula of Jewish casuistic, was a repeal of everything Jewish: "All things are lawful for me" (1 Cor 6.12; cf. 10.23). "Wisdom" gives "freedom," the autonomy of the pneumatic man, who conceives of himself as being free from concrete historical and bodily ties and who elevates himself above the traditional orders of human existence. The real impetus *behind the errors in Corinth*, therefore, was a *misunderstanding of the primitive Christian encounter with the Spirit*.[8] The Pneuma which put total human existence into the exclusive service of the crucified Lord was confused with a supernatural power that transcended natural existence.

c. *The Interrelation Between the Pneumaticism in First and Second Corinthians*

The doctrinal background of the errors under fire in First Corinthians was thus marked by a combination of Jewish tradition and pneumaticism similar to that of Paul's opponents in Second Corinthians. The extensive parallelism

[7] Some in Corinth asserted "that there is no resurrection of the dead" (1 Cor 15.12). That is, they taught that the pneumatic man lives on eternally, but the body, which they despised, would not be resurrected (1 Cor 15.46). This notion led to the gnostic doctrine which is recorded in 2 Tim 2.18: the resurrection has happened already (in baptism)! This doctrine too is not only oriented in opposition to Old Testament-Jewish ideas, but is also developed in precisely those thought patterns.

[8] 1 Cor 2.10-3.1; 12.3; 14.12. The word "pneumatic" occurs fourteen times in 1 Corinthians and only nine times in all the other Pauline epistles together.

in Paul's polemic in both First and Second Corinthians is determined not only by Paul's same base of operation in both cases, that is, his theology of the cross, but also by the two fronts he was facing in each case which were basically and essentially the same. In First Corinthians, Paul contrasts this Pneuma in the congregation, which leads to self-emancipation, with the Spirit that comes from the cross. In Second Corinthians, he contrasts the Pneuma of apostleship which serves self-elevation with the true apostle's conformity to the cross impressed upon him by the Spirit of the crucified: "Let him who boasts, boast of the Lord" (1 Cor 1.31; 2 Cor 10.17). The Jewish background to this whole movement is necessarily more clearly seen in the "clergy" themselves (2 Cor) than it is in the consequences produced by the movement (1 Cor), although these "clergymen" certainly supported the movement with related teaching.

The particulars of the movement fought in Corinth, uncertain in individual details and yet unmistakable in their basic features, are illuminated and confirmed by their religio-historical background and by parallel manifestations essentially related to the movement elsewhere in Paul's mission field.

2. The Religio-Historical Background of Pneumatic Judaism in Corinth

Scholars in the history of religions have shown that the concept of Pneuma under fire in the Corinthian epistles was an essential element of the gnostic world view. "Gnosticism" is the label given by the church fathers to a heretical movement within second-century Christianity. Since the beginning of the twentieth century, thanks largely to the pioneer efforts of Richard Reitzenstein, research in the history of religions has discovered that this Christian heresy was only one branch of a broad religious movement, which also makes its appearance in non-Christian literature. For this reason we now label this entire religious movement as gnosticism, but we must take care to give a more precise evaluation and definition of it. When viewed religio-historically the individual cases where this movement appears present themselves as widely divergent syncretistic mixtures of Oriental mythology and Greek philosophy. By means of *existential analysis*, Hans Jonas[9] discovered that in these instances traditional notions and conceptions were being combined to give expression to a new self-awareness and a new understanding of the world in accordance with man's life situation in late antiquity. The proponents of this religiosity had discovered an authentic self by means of intuitive knowledge which they felt was revelation. This self originated from another, genuinely divine, world and eventually returned to it. Similar to the mystics, they withdrew into this genuine pneumatic self and retreated from corporeal life in this world, which had become the plaything of dubious world rulers. Now traces of this self-awareness can be detected in many places in the environment of primitive Christianity, in magic and the mystery religions as well as in Philo and in the Jewish Baptist movements. From this Bultmann has developed the working hypothesis[10] that in the world about Christianity, even as early as the Pauline era, a well-developed gnostic religiosity was on hand that had considerable effect upon Hellenistic Christianity. From this gnostic religiosity, for example, Christianity borrowed the notion of the descent and ascent of the gnostic redeemer and developed the christology which appears in Phil 2.6-11. However, the last decade of research in history of religions has shown that this hypothesis is untenable, for *in the first century genuine gnosti-*

---

[9] *Gnosis und spätantiker Geist*, I (2d ed.; Göttingen, 1954). *Gnostic Religion* (Boston, 1958).

[10] *Theology*, (Part I, note 1) I, 164ff.

cism, that is, redemptive systems in the gnostic pattern, existed only in a few very isolated places.[11]

The foregoing is made clear if we look into the provenance of the ideas which Paul is combatting in First Corinthians. It is characteristic of these ideas that the self which has been grasped by the redemptive Pneuma despises corporeality and tangible bodily existence. Such a dualism is an essential trait of gnosticism; thus the movement in Corinth represents a preliminary stage of gnosticism, which does not yet contain an expanded system of redemption. But this primitive gnosticism is closely tied to Jewish ideas as we encounter it in Corinth. Where does this close tie stem from? To all appearances it did not stem merely from the Jewish Christians' Hellenistic misconception of the activity of the Spirit, but also from the consequences of a gnostic Judaism; for there is evidence of a considerable volume of gnostic elements already present in pre-Christian Judaism.

a. Gnosticism in Palestinian Judaism

Paul's opponents in Second Corinthians boasted of their Palestinian roots. Within Palestinian Judaism we find no gnostic redemptive system which could be labeled gnosticism strictly speaking, but there are elements of the gnostic world-view. Such elements are at hand in rabbinic speculation about the work of creation and about Ezekiel's vision of the wheels, in the juxtaposition of the heavenly and earthly world by the apocalyptic writers and their heavenly journeys,[12] and above all in the dualism of light and darkness set forth in the famous passage from Qumran (*IQS* 3,13-4,26): "The origin of truth lies in the fountain

[11] R. McL. Wilson, *The Gnostic Problem* (London, 1958). Cf. R. M. Grant, *Gnosticism and Early Christianity* (New York, 1959).

[12] G. Scholem, *Major Trends in Jewish Mysticism* (3d ed.; New York, 1954). *Jewish Gnosticism, Merkabah Mysticism and Talmudic Tradition* (New York, 1960).

of light and that of perversity in the wellspring of darkness" (3.19).[13] The dualistic ideas and forms of expression which we meet here certify that the conceptual vocabulary of the gospel of John as well as that of the Odes of Solomon is rooted in Palestinian Judaism, and that the gnostic Judaism in Corinth also could have its roots there.

b. Samaritan Gnosticism

As an example of gnosticism arising directly within the realm of Jewish religion we may consider *Simon the Magician*. It is probably by no means accidental that his reported reaction to Christianity is connected with the Christians' encounter with the Spirit. According to Acts 8.19, he sought to utilize the Pneuma as a supernatural power at his own disposal in a manner essentially like that of Paul's opposition in Corinth.

In the brief report in Acts, which stands up to serious tests of historicity, we get an exact picture of the nature of this man. He appears in Acts next to Elymas (Acts 13.8) as the most dangerous competitor of the apostles. Both of them, like the apostles, stem from Judaism. Elymas was a Jew, Simon a Samaritan. Like the apostles, they offered present divine redemptive activity which went above and beyond the Old Testament and which appealed to the general longing for redemption characteristic of the age. Before Philip had performed the signs of the gospel in Samaria, Simon had "amazed the nation" with his miracles and won the Samaritans' allegiance. They revered him as "that power of God which is called Great" (Acts 8.10). Just as Jesus was the "power of God" for the believers (1 Cor 1.24), so was Simon for his followers. They saw present in him "that power," in fact, the "Great" power, which transcends all other powers, in short, the highest Godhead.

[13] J. Maier, *Die Texte vom Toten Meer II* (Munich, 1960), pp. 18f. (Bibliography).

176

It was in this sense that he called himself "great" (Acts 8.9). He was a "great one" because he had divine power (Acts 19.27f.). He did not desire to be the Samaritan Messiah or his forerunner; he did not try to fit himself into biblical ideas. His conception of the divine as a power at his disposal placed him beyond the biblical concept of God. Appropriately the New Testament characterizes him as "magician" (Acts 8.9), one who has superhuman power at his disposal by virtue of some secret supernatural knowledge. In the history of religions he belongs to the type called the "divine man."

What Simon himself wished to be, according to the predicates which Acts has preserved, may be drawn from the system of the Simonians[14] encountered by the next generation of the church. Their system expands on these same predicates and therefore to some extent may be traced back to Simon. The most ancient components of the system are those features which are found in analogous form in Menander,[15] who was himself always labeled as a pupil of Simon:

1. According to both, the world was created by angels, who on their part were created by the *ennoia* emanating from the highest Godhead. The angels, however, seized the *ennoia* and confined it to a human body.

2. From then on it wandered from one body to another until Simon discovered it in the harlot Helena in a public house in Tyre and purchased her freedom in order to have the *ennoia* with him from then on. In Simon the highest god (*sublimissima virtus*), himself, unknown to the angels, had appeared in order to reunite his *ennoia* with himself. Purchasing Helena's freedom was most likely a mythical symbol of the redemption Simon accomplished for the divine that was imprisoned in bodily human histori-

[14] Justin, *Apology*, 1.26, and Irenaeus, *Adversus Haereses*, I.23.
[15] Irenaeus, *ibid.*, 1.23.5.

cal existence in order to reunite it with its original source. To be sure, the only things expressly mentioned are the imprisoning of the *ennoia* in this one series of feminine forms and the enslavement of all men under the angelic powers. This incongruity between only one imprisonment and the enslavement of all men arises most likely from the fact that the redemptive idea presented in the system had not yet completely penetrated the historical form in which Simon represented it.

3. Liberation from the dominion of the angelic powers was accomplished by magic in Menander, as it surely also was originally in Simon. Among the Simonians it was *accomplished through knowledge* or through faith in Simon. Anyone thus liberated from the angelic powers no longer needed to bother about the laws given by them.

In Simonianism we have a redemptive system essentially independent of Christianity, but arising on Jewish soil and containing all the basic features of the gnostic system: (1) An explanation of human existence by means of a dualistic cosmogony. (2) The advent of a redeemer from the highest Godhead. Redemption then consists in the extraction (of fallen and incarcerated divinity) from (historical bodily) existence under worldly powers by virtue of connection with the redeemer. Advance demonstrations of such redemption were freedom from the Law and indifference toward anything bodily or historical. (3) Initially the redemption was accomplished by magic, later through knowledge ("gnosis").

c. *The Syncretistic Jewish Gnosticism*

To see the entire extent of gnostic phenomena in the realm of Judaism, however, we must engage in further observation. Besides the incidents of gnosticism in Palestinian Judaism and in Samaria, there was not only Philo's system,[16]

[16] U. Wilckens, *Weisheit und Torheit* (Tübingen, 1959), pp. 139-50.

incorporating numerous gnostic elements, but also the classic pre-Christian gnosticism at the periphery of the Jewish Diaspora. According to Reitzenstein, it was Jews of the first century who had fallen into syncretism in Egypt who wrote the *Poimandres*[17] and Jews in Phrygia at the beginning of the second century who produced the basic text of the *Naassen Sermon*.[18] The author of the former, "the oldest gnostic writing extant," expressed his religiosity in concepts and ideas which he had taken from Iranian traditions, as well as Hellenistic popular philosophy and Plato; but his familiarity with the Old Testament continually shines through. He is probably to be numbered with those Jews bitterly condemned by Philo for following only the allegorical meaning of the Law, but no longer taking it literally. The Christian features of the Naassen Sermon prove to be later additions, but the Old Testament features cannot be skimmed off, thus pointing to the author's provenance in the Jewish Diaspora in Phrygia. If the authors were not themselves of Jewish provenance, they were without question emphatically influenced by Old Testament Jewish ideas. The same is also true of the rest of the documents we know of from non-Christian gnosticism, namely, the *Chaldean oracles*, the oldest strata of *Mandaean* literature, and the *pearl song* in the *Acts of Thomas*. These documents, however, most likely do not go any farther back than the second or third century.[19]

Is it mere coincidence that *the most important in-*

[17] R. Reitzenstein, *Poimandres* (Göttingen, 1904); cf. C. H. Dodd, *The Bible and the Greeks* (2d ed.; London, 1954).

[18] Hippolytus, *Philosophumena* (Refutatio Omnium Haeresium), 5.7. 3-9.9. R. Reitzenstein (note 17), pp. 83-93.

[19] A good survey of recent research is found in S. Schulz, "Die Bedeutung der neuen Gnosisfunde für die ntl. Wissenschaft," *ThR*, XXVI (1960), 209-66, 301-34. New light has also been thrown upon the origins and nature of gnosticism by the discovery of a large number of Christian-gnostic manuscripts at Nag Hammadi. See W. C. van Unnik, *Newly Discovered Gnostic Writings* (London, 1960).

stances of non-Christian gnosticism which historians have unearthed up till now all *have grown on soil significantly influenced by Judaism?* Judaism actually seems to have taken an active role in *the rise and development of gnosticism.* With reference to its conceptual vocabulary gnosticism grew out of a blend of Iranian and Babylonian religion with Hellenistic philosophy. The power which gave shape to the movement was the gnostic understanding of existence and the corresponding longing of the Oriental man of late antiquity for redemption. Under these circumstances what sort of role could have fallen to Judaism? That Judaism which inclined toward syncretism was an ideal meeting-ground for the major motifs. In Judaism, Iranian-Babylonian ideas and the Greek thought-world could easily engage each other under the rubric of this particular understanding of existence. In addition it could also make a material contribution to formulating the gnostic message of redemption. Judaism was cordial to the idea of redemption through a universal redemptive message originating in ancient traditions and to the impetus for this idea, namely, the lumping together of all other divinations into second-class gods distinguished from the highest Godhead. We shall conclude with one last piece of evidence, namely, the anti-Jewish attitude of later gnosticism which initially seems to speak against any affinity between Judaism and gnosticism. This antithesis can be explained precisely from this developmental affinity. That Judaism which leaned toward syncretism and mysticism stood in opposition to official nomistic Judaism from the very outset. This opposition intensified particularly after A.D. 70 in view of official Judaism's anathema on heretics, the growing anti-Semitism which animated the age, and the additional antithesis of the Christian church. This opposition did not prevent Jewish tradition from having significant effect on the for-

180

mative growth of gnosticism,[20] as can already be shown by the gnostic systems within heretical Jewish Christianity that arose after 70.[21] In them we have a visual illustration of the gnostic Judaism of Paul's time.

The proportions and power of Jewish gnosticism as well as its affinity to Christianity help us understand why *Paul gave more room in his letters to a defense against gnostic Judaism* than he did against the nomistic strain. Gnostic Judaism, after all, united in itself exactly those features which spoke to the religious needs of wider circles of people. The battle taken up in the letters to the Corinthians is most likely continued in the brief warnings in Phil 3 and Rom 16, and is very clearly carried forward in Colossians and in the Pastorals.

3. *The Warnings in Philippians 3 and Romans 16*

Because of their brevity the sharp warnings[22] in Phil 3.2,18f. are not without ambiguity. Their content and context are more reminiscent of Second Corinthians than of Galatians. Here too there are "workers," missionizing teachers (Phil 3.2; cf. 2 Cor 11.13). Here too there is a boasting about Jewish advantages (Phil 3.4-6; cf. 2 Cor 11.22) in connection with a perfectionism (Phil 3.12; cf. 1

[20] In the time that has elapsed since this book first appeared most scholars in history of religions have come to concur in the insight that Jewish influences alongside of Iranian-Oriental mythology and Greek philosophy constitute a necessary third factor in the rise of gnosticism. R. McL. Wilson (note 11) has now supplied the comprehensive documentation. Accordingly gnosticism arose only on the periphery of Judaism and Christianity. This occurred at several places simultaneously since about the middle of the first century.

[21] The most significant documents of a gnostic Jewish Christianity in the second century are the book of Elchasai and the Kerygmata Petru, a source document for the [Pseudo-] Clementine Homilies and Recognitions. E. Hennecke, *Neutestamentliche Apokryphen* (3d ed. by W. Schnecmelcher; Tübingen, 1964), pp. 63-80, 529-32. English translation, *New Testament Apocrypha*, Vol. II, ed. by R. McL. Wilson.

[22] Cf. the New Testament introductions and the commentaries on the warnings in Philippians 3 and Romans 16.

Cor 4.8) and a worldly self-centeredness (Phil 3.17ff.). Here too Paul contrasts confidence in the flesh (Phil 3.3) with "exclusive longing for the knowledge of Jesus" and "the love which shares Jesus' sufferings" (Schlatter) (Phil 3.10). The adversaries also emphasize circumcision (Phil 3.2; cf. 19)—something which is not said of the opponents in Corinth—but only as their own personal advantage, not as a demand on the whole congregation. They could not have been, as was long assumed, nomistic Judaizers. Among many others, Lohmeyer[23] thought that Phil 3.2 referred to Jewish agitators who had brought persecution on the congregation (Phil 1.28ff.) and put pressure on the Christians to fall away. But these statements obviously do not belong in the same category as those in 1 Thess 2.14ff.; Rev. 2.9; 3.9, but rather in the category of 2 Cor 10-13 and the passage in Rom 16.17-20, which most surely speaks of enticers who are themselves Christians. Since there is evidently no internal danger to congregational life (Phil 1.3ff.), the polemic in Philippians as well as that in Rom 16.17-20, which is almost word for word the same, is probably a precautionary warning against a threat to the church which is making itself felt in many places.

4. Judaizing "Element" Philosophy in Colossae[24]

In the pretentious brand of Christianity against which Colossians is directed, only a few essential features can be apprehended by which Paul demonstrates its incompatibility with the gospel. Characteristic throughout is an oscillation between the Jewish and the Hellenistic provenance of these features: commandments that correspond literally to Mosaic laws and yet have a completely different meaning, powers that are designated as angels and yet belong to

---

[23] In the Meyer-Kommentar series (1930), ad loc. According to Lohmeyer, Phil 3.17-21 is directed against apostate Christians.

[24] E. Percy, Die Probleme der Kolosser und Epheserbriefe (Lund, 1946), pp. 137-78. G. Bornkamm, "Die Häresie des Kolosserbriefes," in Das Ende des Gesetzes (Munich, 1952).

an unbiblical cosmology, and an appeal to tradition that allows the wellsprings of Hellenism to stream in under this Jewish principle.

In Colossae the congregation is required to keep ordinances relating to food and drink, festivals, new moons, and sabbaths (Col 2.16). These ordinances are unmistakably connected with Mosaic laws. Only for that reason can Paul designate these pious practices as a "shadow" of the Christian worship service (Col 2.17). And yet at the same time he can call them mere "human precepts" (Col 2.22), for they are no longer Old Testament commandments. They have a different meaning. Here particular foods were forbidden not to insure obedience to Levitical purity, but rather to avoid the danger inherent in matter and to escape the spell of one's own body. Thus observing the days may also have had a cosmic significance. Such practices bring "honor" (2.23), blessing from the deity, perhaps "visions" (2.18), and a "fullness" (2.9)—but they actually serve only for man's own self-elevation.

Such an interpretation of the significance of these ordinances corresponds to the foundation upon which they were based. Here the *difference from the Judaizers in Galatia* becomes particularly clear. Galatians proclaims Christ as the end of the Law, Colossians as the conquest of the *stoicheia*, the elemental spirits of the universe (Col 2.8,20f.). In Galatians Paul polemically equates servitude to the law with the pre-Christian world under the elements of the universe (Gal 4.3,9); in Colossians the heresy itself justifies its ordinances by reference to the "elemental spirits of the universe." In the former the goal is to be righteous before God, in the latter, to influence the cosmos. The former deals with nomistic Judaism, the latter with syncretistic Judaism.

What did the Colossians understand by the "*elemental spirits of the universe*"? That which is done for the sake of the elemental spirits is designated "worship of angels" (Col 2.18). But in keeping with the meaning of the ordinances the elemental spirits here are not angels in the Jewish sense, mediators of God's will, but rather personifications of the basic elements or the stars which have come forth from the "deity" (cf. Col 2.10) and now stand between it and men. The religio-historical background is not Jewish hypostasizing of God's pronouncements, but rather Iranian worship of the elements. Most likely the elemental spirits were not thought of as the tyrants of the lower world, but rather as emanations from the "fullness" of the deity. In the first case asceticism would be a means to be liberated from them, and in the second case a means to attain relationship with them. The worship of angels is accordingly either identical to asceticism or a mystery cult connected with it.

Paul's polemic leaves all of this open, since for him only one thing matters: the elemental spirits of the universe in any case belong to the cosmic powers (Col 2.10; 15). Christ, however, is not to be classified together with these, as the Colossians tried to do.[25] As the one and only eschatological mediator of salvation, He has actually deposed them. In Christ alone is to be found everything which the Colossians were vainly seeking to find above Him and beside Him (Col 2.3,9,11,17,20).

With reference to its provenance this teaching represented itself as "tradition" (Col 2.8), something both Jews and Gentiles loved, a revealed and transmitted esoteric doctrine. But to Paul it was only "human tradition," a human creation! It wanted to be philosophy (Col 2.8,23) in the Hellenistic sense, a speculative view resting on revelation and tradition. For Paul this "philosophy" was "empty deceit," a futile work of autocratic human thought. Since all wisdom and knowledge are hidden in Christ, all that really matters is to know His mystery (Col 2.2f.).

The element philosophy in Colossae tried to transform

[25] In Elchasai's vision of revelation (note 21) Christ and the Spirit appear as angels. At baptism one is to call on the elements. In other respects, too, the Judaizing gnosticism of the Book of Elchasai illustrates notions against which Colossians polemicizes.

184

what was offensive and foolish into something that Jews and Gentiles desired. The teaching emphatically and consciously connected itself to Jewish tradition. Its proponents did not come, like the Corinthian pneumatics, from Palestine, but probably from the centuries-old Diaspora in Phrygia, which was considerably infected with syncretism. What was offered as Christian under this Jewish label was actually nothing but Hellenistic syncretism. The essential features of the teaching already discussed gave expression to a dualistic system of redemption whose terminology allows it to be regarded as gnostic. The element philosophy in Colossae was *gnostic Judaism*. The intrinsically related phenomenon in the same church territory which was the target for the polemics in the Pastoral Letters expressly declares itself to be gnosticism.

5. The "Falsely Called Gnosis" in the Pastoral Letters

The Pastoral Letters fight a type of Christianity in the congregations of the province of "Asia" (1 Tim 1.3), and on the isle of Crete (Tit 1.5ff.) which calls itself "gnosis" (gnosticism) (1 Tim 6.20). Since the conditions surrounding the origin of the Pastoral Letters are still being debated today, the clues for establishing the *historical place of this phenomenon* will have to be gotten first from their own content. Individual features will emerge if we compare related movements in the same church territory against which the Letter to the Colossians and Ignatius protest.

The error did not yet appear as a school of thought with a definite system of teaching. It was represented as independent charismatic teaching, which elicited discussion in the congregational assemblies and was carried into the homes as private instruction (2 Tim 2.23, 3.6ff.). The *promoters of the movement*, usually designated with the very general term "certain persons," stemmed for the most part from the "circumcision party" (Tit 1.10). They desired to be "teachers of the law" (1 Tim 1.7), Christian scribes, who by their exegesis of the scripture would show the congregation the way to understand the faith and above all the proper way of life (1 Tim 1.8-11; Tit 3.9). From among the *legalistic regulations* which they gave, it is mentioned that they forbade certain foods and marriage (1 Tim 4.3; Tit 1.14f.). The latter regulation clearly betrayed the unbiblical character of these ordinances. It contradicted the Old Testament Law and belongs in the realm of Hellenistic dualism. Thus the abstinence from food, here as in Colossae, served as "bodily training" (1 Tim 4.8). In spite of their connection to the Old Testament Law, the regulations here as well as in Colossae were no longer Old Testament commands of God, but rather "commands of men" (Tit 1.14).

In similar fashion the *accompanying speculations* on which these commands were based are characterized as "myths and endless genealogies" (1 Tim 1.4; 4.7; Tit 3.9). In Tit 1.14 the myths are designated "Jewish." They were Jewish first because of their derivation, then also because of their content and its origin. They were derived from the scripture with scribal skill. The genealogies were not gnostic chains of eons, but rather family trees of mankind. The expression as a whole probably meant the expositions of the Old Testament, especially the primeval history, following the Jewish Haggada and aiming toward a gnostic cosmogony and anthropogony. As far as their actual content was concerned, these interpretations were profane fables equal to heathen histories of the gods.[26] The whole character of these speculations was illuminated by the central statement: "The resurrection is past already" (2 Tim 2.18). In a perfectionistic sense the resurrection was already present in the pneumatic experience. Even the first appearance of this movement in Corinth closely approached this central statement.[27] This devaluation of the body opened the door to

[26] Stählin's article μῦθος, TWNT, IV, 789ff.
[27] See note 7.

self-redemption via either ascetic or libertine attitudes and took from God the honor of being the one who creates out of nothing (Rom 4.17).

In its total character, therefore, this phenomenon was gnosticism in accordance with its own self-designation "gnosis" (1 Tim 6.20). The word was not yet used here as a party label, but as a technical term. "Gnosis" meant to know God's reality by revelation, and thereby to have re-demption.[28] But this gnosis still wore a Jewish robe. Its relationship to Jewish tradition was relatively weaker than that of the syncretistic Judaizers in Corinth and Colossae, but completely different from that of the "Judaizers" con-demned by Ignatius. With Ignatius, "Judaizing" was a polemical reproach against a teaching propounded by Gen-tile Christians which doted on speculative interpretation of the scripture and legalistic regulations without itself making any appeal to Jewish tradition.[29] In the Pastoral Letters a connection with Jewish tradition was still an advantage, and the Jewish Christians who promoted the "gnosis" flattered themselves with the fact that their teaching had this con-nection. After the year 70 such a connection became less and less a recommendation to Hellenistic men; but this pejorative character of the designation "Jewish" cannot yet be detected in the Pastoral Letters. After the close of the first century, docetism, to which gnosticizing devaluation of the body had now led, became the focus of the church's controversy with gnosis. But there is also as yet no indica-tion of this situation in the Pastoral Letters, although it appears in 1 John as well as in Ignatius and Polycarp. These two important observations indicate that the "different doc-trine" fought in the Pastoral Letters belongs in the realm of

[28] The Greek word "gnosis" is used in the same way in the hermetic literature (cf. Bultmann's article γιγνώσκω, TWNT, I, 692ff.). In the New Testament the first such occurrence is in 1 Corinthians (TWNT, I, 709f.).

[29] Ignatius, Philad., 6.1; Mag. 8.1.

Judaistic gnosticism, which is no longer to be found in the Greek church after the close of the Pauline era.

The *manner in which the battle is fought in the Pastorals* also corresponds to the chronological place we have assigned to them. In their opposition to gnosticism they appeal for faithfulness to transmitted apostolic truth.[30] This is more formalistic than the authoritative Christ-centered counterblows in Corinthians and Colossians, but in contrast to Ignatius' mobilizing the ecclesiastical organization, it is still in keeping with the method of the apostles. It is *the manner of the pupils of the apostles*, as Luke, for example, typifies. In important basic principles of defense the Pastoral Letters coincide with Paul: senseless discussion about this "interpretation of the scripture" is rejected. The false teachers are characterized according to their overall attitude; they are men of shattered faith who use the gospel as a means for elevating themselves, especially in the most elementary way, money-making.[31] The positive defense against them is the "economy of God," administering the entrusted goods in the service of God for the edification of the church (1 Tim 1.4).

In our attempt to determine the historical place of the "different doctrine" referred to in the Pastoral Letters, we have come across signs of the *close of the epoch* just described in the relationship between Christianity and Judaism. The church emerging from Judaism is accompanied by a double threat from Judaism. In nomistic Judaizing it threatens, like the dragon in Rev 12, to devour the emerging church, and in gnostic Judaizing it threatens to inundate the church in the flood of syncretism cast out behind it. The basic change which came in all these connections with Judaism in post-Pauline times characterized the close of this epoch as a first important turning-point in the primitive history of the church and its theology.

[30] 1 Tim 4.6; 6.3,14,20; 2 Tim 1.12ff.; 2.1f.,8; 3.10,14.
[31] 1 Tim 1.5f.,19f.; 4.2; 6.4f.,21; Tit 1.11.

CONCLUSION

Chapter XIV

Outlook for Subsequent Development

In the decade between 60 and 70 drastic historical events brought the first epoch in the history of primitive Christianity to a conclusion and introduced a second one. Each of the three leading men of the first epoch, James the Lord's brother, Paul, and Peter met a martyr's death one right after the other between 62 and 64. In Rome for the first time the eyes of the imperial public were turned upon the Christians. Up until this time in the Roman world the Christians were generally considered a Jewish sect, but now it became apparent that they were a new and independent religious fellowship. It was only Christians, not Jews, whom Nero officially persecuted and publicly punished in the fall of 64. Their reputation was already of such a nature that people believed them capable of wanting to destroy the world metropolis with fire. A long and complicated conflict began between the church and the empire and imperial society. In the year 66 the Jewish people in Palestine, antagonized by the arbitrary action of the Roman procurator and deluded by the messianic dreams of the Zealots, arose in a hopeless revolt against the Roman world empire. In crushing the revolt, the Romans devastated the land and finally in the year 70 destroyed Jerusalem and the Temple. The Jewish revolt caused the Christian church in Palestine to be scattered. The remnants who assembled afterward in the devastated land were no longer of any significance for the Gentile Christian church between Antioch and Rome. What the Gentile Christians lost by this event was that living tie with Old Testament Jewish tradition which re-

189

sisted any deifying of the divine, any attempt to confuse the creator with anything in the creation. Judaism itself, however, was reassembled after the catastrophe and structured by Pharisaic scribalism. It withdrew from its missionary task to the world and entrenched itself behind the walls of the Law. Around the year 80 the curse formula upon the *Minim*, especially the Jewish Christians, was inserted into the Prayer of Eighteen Petitions and therewith Jewish Christians were expelled once and for all from the Jewish folk community. However, this did not prevent Judaism from exerting further strong influence upon the church through its literature (e.g., the Apocalypses) and through oral tradition. This took place all the more readily since the church now stood in a situation similar to that of Judaism after the Babylonian Exile.

Up until the Pauline era the church's primary task was achieving independence from Judaism. Judaism, however, had simultaneously been the shell that protectively surrounded the initial growth of the church. But now *Christianity had to assert itself on its own in the world of Hellenistic culture* where syncretism was the working principle. This was the task facing the second apostolic generation. Their fulfilling this task had been materially aided by the preparatory work of the missionary confrontation with Hellenism in the Pauline era and especially by Paul's own battle with Judaizing gnosticism. Judaizing gnosticism had solved the problem of Christianity and syncretism by Hellenizing Christianity. In his battle with this gnosticism *Paul had developed theological assertions on Hellenistic Christian soil* which continued to influence decisively the further shape of the church and its message even if the apostle's theology as such was not directly utilized in the next era. The most primitive *christological formulation* had confessed: Jesus "was descended from David according to the flesh and designated Son of God in power according to the

Spirit of holiness by his resurrection from the dead" (Rom 1.3f.). In the Hellenistic world, especially in confrontation with gnosticism, Jesus had to be brought into connection with the cosmos. One precipitate of this was the pre-existence christology, whose creed we see reflected in 1 Cor 8.6 and expanded in Col 1.13-20: "As indeed there are many 'gods' and many 'lords,' yet for us there is one God, the Father, from whom are all things and for whom we exist, and one Lord, Jesus Christ, through whom are all things and through whom we exist." As soon as the question was raised about Jesus' relationship to the cosmos, the confession had to be made: Jesus does not belong on the side of creation and the world powers, but on the side of the creator; the mediator of the new world is also the mediator of the first creation! *Pre-existence christology* did not develop as an amateurish transfer of mythical ideas onto Jesus, but it was an existential confession, which naturally made use of available means of expression. At the same time Jesus' work of redemption, which Romans interprets as justification in reference to Law and promise, is now proclaimed as the disarming of the world powers: Christ liberates from the powers of fate (Phil 2.9ff.; Col 2.15). In keeping with this christological and soteriological confession the believer regulated his *ethical relationship* to his own body and to corporeal historical life. Gnosticism fluctuated between libertinism and asceticism and proved also in this ethical respect to be a failure in seeking to regulate the relationship of Christianity to the Hellenistic world. In contrast to this Paul in First Corinthians formulated the following fundamental statements valid for all time: "Your bodies are members of Christ" (1 Cor 6.15) and "everyone should remain in the state in which he was called," e.g., in the estate of marriage (1 Cor 7.20). In Colossians this fundamental assertion was expanded into the earliest New Testament "social code" (3.18-4.1). These ethical directives, like the christological confessions, were not isolated assertions occurring only once in these particular letters, but instead they constituted *binding tradition* for the church. Their stylized form already betrays that fact, although the apostle himself had authoritatively shaped them. In similar fashion assertions about *the church* had to be fashioned and extended. In the language of biblical redemptive history the church was "the seed of Abraham" and "the Israel of God," but for Hellenistic thought it had to be interpreted as the "body of Christ" and in connection with that another side of its essence, its pneumatic character, had to be articulated more clearly (1 Cor 10.17; 12; Col 1.18; Eph 1.23). With reference to the church, baptism and the Lord's Supper as well as the role and duty of those in church offices needed further clarification. Last but not least, *eschatology* had to be rephrased and refounded in the categories of the Hellenistic world. As is evident in First Corinthians, gnosticism in its earliest stages had abandoned eschatology insofar as it amounted to an expectation of the future end; and insofar as eschatology expressed the presence of salvation, gnosticism had transformed it into ecstatic enthusiasm (1 Cor 4.8).

In the hour of the church's emergence from Judaism and its entrance into the Hellenistic world Paul had rendered the crucial service of seeing that both occurred in a manner that was theologically defensible. How the church would fashion her life and message in this world and how to maintain them were the problems which the second generation (A.D. 70 to 100) had to solve and did solve in a way that was also fundamental for all subsequent ages. However, it was the church's first generation in its controversy and conflict with Judaism that laid the irreplaceable foundation for building the church and fashioning its message. The relationship between Christianity and Judaism was the central problem of Christianity's theology and the church's existence in the first generation and for all time.

192